Black Man's Tears

*A Poetic Witness to Invisibility,
Inheritance, and Becoming*

JOHN DAVID SMITH

Scribe & Canvas Publishing
South Carolina

Paperback ISBN: 979-8-9995975-4-0
Library of Congress Control Number: 2025944882

Published by Scribe & Canvas Publishing™
Pendleton, SC | www.scribeandcanvas.com

Interior and cover design by Elev8d Designs
Printed in the United States of America

10 9 8 7 6 5 4 3 2 1

To the Black men who cry in silence,
stand in shadows,
and carry more than this world will ever know—
your tears are not weakness.
They are sacred.
They are soil.
They are song.

To the fathers who stayed,
the sons who searched,
the brothers who broke
and still believed—
this is for you.

And to the ancestors
whose prayers held me
long before I had the words—
I am your echo.
I am your witness.
I am still becoming.

The Poet's Prelude

The Black Man's Tears is not just a collection of
poems—it is a body.
A body that remembers.
That weeps.
That kneels in protest and prayer.

These verses rose from the marrow of combined
stories,
shaped by the echoes of our ancestors,
the weight of Black manhood,
and the fire of faith that refused to be silenced.

I wrote this not to be profound,
but to be present.
To witness.
To heal.

This collection flows in five parts—mirroring the body
of a sermon,
the structure of a life,
the journey of a soul.

From identity and innocence,
to pain and prophecy,
from the burden of manhood
to the beauty of redemption—
every poem is a step.
A wound.
A whisper.

A war cry.

These poems live their own life.
They speak not only for me,
but for those who came before—
men like Rev. Dr. Martin Luther King Jr., Malcolm X,
and Nelson Mandela—
and for those whose names have become rallying cries:
Rodney King, George Floyd, Daunte Wright,
and countless others whose stories echo in our bones.

Fathers, sons, brothers, ministers, strangers.
Survivors.

So I invite you—
to enter these pages with open hands and honest
questions.
You may not find answers.
But you will find truth.
And truth, when spoken from a trembling place,
can still set us free.

Let this book be a mirror,
a map,
and a mercy.
For the ones who still rise—
even when the world gives them every reason not to.

This book is not meant to be rushed.
Each poem carries its own weight,
its own story,
its own truth.
I invite you to take your time—
pause between the lines,
breathe between the pages,

and let the words settle.

These poems are not just meant to be read;
they are meant to be felt,
reflected upon,
and carried with you.

Whether you read one poem at a time
or immerse yourself in a section,
let the journey unfold at your own pace.

Healing, witnessing, and becoming
are not hurried acts—
they are sacred ones.

— *John David Smith*

Table of Contents

In the Mirror

Before the world told me who I was,
I was already becoming—
in whispers, in wounds,
in the names I dared to answer.

◐

Before They Called Me Boy

I was a breath before the bruise,
laughter braided in the wind,
still humming the songs
that my great-grandmother
once whispered to the river.

Back then,
I was all sky—
my skin didn't yet speak
before others spoke for it.
My hands only knew mud and mango,
not how to carry suspicion
in their open palms.

They hadn't yet shrunk my name
into something that echoed shame,
hadn't polished me down
to a shadow in a store window,
hadn't told me to lower my voice
before I learned its thunder.

I remember
the way light bent toward me then—
not out of fear,
but welcome.
I remember
the way my mother looked at me
like I was a prophecy
walking on small feet.

Before they called me boy,
I was becoming a world
that believed itself whole.
And then—
a silence wrapped around me
that I did not choose.

The Skin I Live In

This skin—
brown as dirt after rain,
as bark holding the memory of fire—
was never a question
until someone answered it
without asking me.

I remember the first time
I saw myself
through someone else's gaze—
a teacher's narrowed eyes,
a stranger's clutching purse,
a boy at recess
who asked if I was dirty
or just "that color."

They said,
speak clearly,
stand straight,
don't scare them.
As if my voice
and my spine
and my presence
were warnings,
not wonders.

But this skin
has danced before it crawled,
prayed before it sinned,

bled in silence
and still bore fruit.
It holds stories
my mouth hasn't dared to tell.

Sometimes,
I wish I could unzip it,
just for a moment,
to see who I'd be
without the weight of interpretation.
But then I think
of my grandfather's hands—
cracked but steady,
the same shade as mine.

And I remember:
I come from earth
that loved the sun too much
to stay pale.

What My Name Wasn't

They called me "boy"
before they learned my name—
as if manhood was theirs to grant,
a currency I hadn't earned yet.

They tried to rename me
with their tongues
that stumbled over syllables
not made in their mouths.
Turned Malik into "Mal,"
Kofi into "Coffee,"
Elijah into "Eli,"
until my heritage
sounded like a convenience.

I answered to what they gave me
until I stopped recognizing myself
in the echo.

See, a name is a seed—
a whisper from the womb,
a prophecy in syllables.
My mother gave me mine
with prayer-stained lips,
my father etched it
in the wood of a cradle
he never slept beside.
But I carried it—
even when it felt too heavy,

too strange,
too Black
for school roll calls
and job interviews.

I learned to say it slow,
like a scripture.
To spell it out
like a spell.
To hear it called
and know the ancestors
were still listening.

My name is not
a favor you do me.
It is not an apology
on your tongue.
It is a door I open
every time I speak.

That Time I First Cried in Public

It wasn't the fall
that cracked me open—
not the scrapes,
not the sting of gravel
pressed into skin
like Braille from the ground.

It was the laugh.
Sharp.
Sudden.
From someone I trusted
to wipe tears, not tally them.

I was seven,
maybe eight—
young enough to cry honest,
old enough to know
the world had rules
for boys like me.

My lip trembled like a preacher's first prayer,
but I swallowed the sob—
halfway.
Just enough to make it sour
before it spilled.
I remember the color of the sky,

a cracked chalk blue,
and the silence after,
so loud it stunned the birds.

"Man up,"
someone said,
as if manhood
was measured in silence
and tear ducts were sin.

I did.
I stood.
Wiped salt from my cheeks
with the back of my hand
like it was shame.

But something changed.
That day, I learned
how to cry without water,
how to ache behind the eyes,
how to press pain
into the folds of my pocket
like lint.

I carried that
for years—
until the weight
became a language.

Barbershop Baptism

It smelled like clippers,
old spice,
sweat-stuck leather
and Friday night jokes
that stretched through generations
like a hymn hummed low.

I was too small for the chair,
so they stacked me on a booster,
a throne of cracked vinyl
and wobbling faith.

The cape went around my neck
like a preacher's robe,
tight but holy.
The clippers buzzed,
and I flinched—
not from fear,
but from the weight of watching men
become.

There were mirrors everywhere,
each one telling me
I was no longer just a boy.

A man behind me sculpted silence
into a lineup,
shaped my crown with calloused hands
that had carried stories

from heads bowed
in pain,
in prayer,
in pride.

Each pass of the blade
cut deeper than hair—
stripping play from my face,
sanding down softness
until only shape remained.

The old heads watched,
nodding with slow approval.
No words, just knowing.
As if they saw the shadow of manhood
fall across my brow
for the first time.

When it was done,
I looked at myself
and didn't know the boy.

I walked out
new.
Not baptized in water,
but edged into being
by the buzz and hum
of becoming.

My Mother's Prayers Had Elbows

My mother never prayed
with soft hands.
Her prayers had elbows—
sharp, sure,
knocking through heaven's ribs
to stir the angels.

She never folded her hands
like a postcard saint.
She *gripped* them—
tight as the steering wheel
when we slid on black ice,
tight as the broom
when the rent was late
and dignity was swept into corners.

I once saw her in the dark,
shoulders heaving,
knees bruised on the linoleum
like she was wrestling
not with God,
but *for* Him—
to show up
before the lights were cut again.

She spoke in tongues I didn't learn

in Sunday school.
Groans.
Choked hallelujahs.
Scriptures sewn
between "Lord, I need You,"
and
"Don't let my son go under."

When I slept,
she watched.
Not hovering,
but guarding—
a lioness with holy breath.

She laid hands on my head
when I didn't know what I was becoming.
She cast out every doubt
before it had the nerve
to settle.

And now—
when I pray,
it's not her words I borrow,
but her *stance*.
Back straight,
heart forward,
faith like a blade in her hand.

Her prayers had elbows—
and I'm still
being nudged
by every one.

I Wasn't Always This Tired

I used to run just to run—
barefoot, breathless,
through the steam of summer streets
where chalk drawings outlasted dreams.
The wind knew my name
back then.
So did the trees.

I laughed loud enough
to shake dust from the porch rails,
louder than the sermons
spilled from secondhand televisions.
My joy was a gospel
no one taught me—
but I knew every note.

I wasn't always this tired.

There was a time
when sleep meant nothing
but a pause between possibilities,
and my bones didn't carry
so many echoes.
Every fall
was a lesson in rising,
not a reminder of what might break.

The world hadn't yet told me
I was too much—

too dark,
too soft,
too slow to hate.

I trusted hands then.
Even strangers'.
Believed in promises
wrapped in candy wrappers
and Sunday shoes.

I wasn't always this tired.

Back before I learned
to read between silences,
before eyes looked away
when I entered a room,
before the questions
always carried
an answer too heavy to say.

Before fear
was stitched into my shadow.
Before I had to earn
the right to just be.

There was once
a boy—
light-footed,
wild-hearted,
woundless.
He lives in my chest still,
sometimes kicking
to remind me
that I wasn't always this tired.

The Mirror in My Grandfather's Hallway

It hung like a sentinel
in that narrow stretch between bedrooms—
gilded frame, edges dulled
from decades of passing palms
and whispered glances.

I was never tall enough
to meet it head-on.
Always the bottom half—
knees, belt buckle,
a slice of chin
if I stood on tiptoe.

That mirror held ghosts
with good posture.
Men who never slouched,
women with pressed blouses
and eyes that had seen
the inside of too many prayers.

Grandfather walked by it
like it knew something.
Paused sometimes
as if checking to see
if time had remembered his face.
I caught myself there once—

after running,
sweat glistening
like revelation on my brow—
and thought:
this glass
does not lie,
but it does not speak.

It never told me
what kind of man I'd become.
Never warned me
that reflection is a language
you must grow old to read.

But still, it offered something—
a place to see
where the world ends
and I begin.
A silver silence
that measured how much
of my father's nose I carried,
how much of my mother's
softness hid behind my stare.

And in time,
I learned to meet it—
eye to eye,
heart to silence,
boy to myth—
in the hush of that hallway
where lineage and light
met without flinching.

Black Boy Running

I ran because I could—
feet slick with summer,
lungs full of after-school light,
the wind folding around me
like a secret I hadn't yet outgrown.

Sometimes it was tag.
Sometimes it was nothing at all—
just the joy of outpacing stillness,
of beating my own shadow
to the edge of the block.

But other times—
it was sirens.
It was a yell from across the street.
It was the gaze that stuck
like gum to the sole of my sneakers.

I didn't know I was running
for my life
until I was.

Didn't know the difference
between play and panic
until I reached a corner
and had to choose
which street didn't look
like a question I couldn't answer.
There's a kind of running

Black boys learn
without instruction—
a sprint stitched
into the seams of our childhood,
a bolt taught by instinct,
by news clippings,
by whispers in the kitchen
when they think we're asleep.

We run not to escape—
but to remember
that our bodies can move
before they're marked,
before they're mistaken.

I ran
until the world blurred,
until breath became a drum,
until every slap of pavement
said I'm still here,
still moving,
still mine.

They Said I Was Too Quiet

They mistook my silence
for absence.
As if words were the only way
to prove you're alive.

I listened
more than I spoke—
not because I lacked the tongue
but because I heard
what others swallowed.

In corners,
I built cathedrals from glances,
translated sighs into scripture,
read the hymns between
a mother's tired footsteps
and a father's empty chair.

They said,
"That boy too quiet,"
and meant:
We don't know what he's hiding.
As if stillness were a mask
and not a mirror.

But my quiet was never empty.
It was gathering—
cloud before storm,
seed before bloom.

I memorized the pauses in stories,
the weight of unspoken names,
the color of fear in a teacher's voice
when the lesson turned toward truth.

I could tell you what wasn't said
and what it meant.

Even now,
I speak like someone
who has studied the art of silence—
who knows that some truths
refuse to be loud.

They said I was too quiet.
But I was always listening—
even when they weren't.

Alphabet of Survival

A is for Always
keep your hands where they can see them—
even if they ain't looking for you,
they're looking through you.

B is for Boy—
but not for long.
They'll make a man out of you
before your voice catches up.

C is for Code-switching:
tongue tucked behind teeth,
slang replaced with sir and smile,
the art of translation
without ever being heard.

D is for Don't—
don't run,
don't stare,
don't reach,
don't dream too loud.

E is for Eyes—
yours open,
theirs watching.

F is for Fear
you're taught to wear like skin—
not loud, not proud,

but stitched beneath the Sunday best.

G is for God—
who sees you,
even when they refuse to.

H is for History
you carry like a second spine—
rigid, unseen,
broken in places you can't pronounce.

I is for Invisible—
until you aren't,
until you are
the threat in the room.

J is for Jump—
at loud sounds,
at sirens,
at sudden silence.

K is for Knees—
your father's on the floor,
your ancestors' in the field,
yours learning to bend
and not break.

L is for Learn—
not just school,
but streets,
and silence,
and survival.

M is for Mama
who teaches you all of this

before you ever know
how to spell it.

And the rest?
You live it.
Every letter,
every lesson
etched not on paper
but on bone.

First Sunday Suit

They pressed it like prophecy—
creased and clean,
as if starch could straighten
what the world might bend.

The jacket swallowed my shoulders,
sleeves grazing knuckles
not yet calloused,
but already burdened.

It smelled of mothballs and sanctified hope,
borrowed pride stitched in every seam.
A hand-me-down from a cousin
who no longer believed in altars.

Mama knelt before me,
tightened my tie like she was praying—
each tug a plea
that I be seen, but not too clearly.

She said,
Walk like you know somebody's watching.
Stand like you belong in the story.
Smile, even if your shoes pinch.

And I did—
I stood in that pew
like a framed picture,
a boy disguised as promise.

The elders nodded their approval,
called me "young man"
like it was both blessing
and demand.

But I remember
how that suit itched—
how the fabric of expectation
chafed beneath my skin,
how holiness felt heavy
when worn too early.

Still, I wore it.
Because to be dressed
was to be worthy
of God,
of man,
of survival.

The Bruise on My Bicycle

It was a red bike with rust in its breath,
bought secondhand but ridden like a dream—
until the curb taught me
how asphalt remembers skin.

I didn't cry when the metal kissed my knee,
when gravel buried itself in soft places.
I just stared at the blood,
like it was a new language
my body had suddenly learned to speak.

The bruise came later—
midnight purple,
blossoming slow across my thigh
like something sacred and ugly
all at once.

Mama dabbed it with peroxide,
her silence louder than the fizz.
She didn't say,
That's what happens when you fall.
She just said,
Next time, don't forget to brake.

But the lesson was bigger
than handlebars and timing.
It was in how I stood up,
shaking but unbroken,
how I checked the bike

before I checked myself.

I learned that pain don't always mean pause—
sometimes, it means
ride different,
watch the road,
carry the bruise like a badge.

Even now,
when life throws me
into curbs I didn't see coming,
I remember that red bike,
how it never apologized,
just waited for me
to get back on.

Shoelaces and Silence

He never taught me to tie them.
I learned from watching other boys—
their fingers a ballet of knowing,
pull, loop, tuck, tighten—
while mine fumbled in the hush
he left behind.

Mama said it wasn't a big deal,
that shoes are meant for walking, not grieving.
But I knew better.
Each knot I tied was a question
he never stayed long enough to answer.

On days when the world came undone,
I blamed the loose strings.
Double-knotted them like prayers,
as if tightness could stand in
for touch.
Some men leave with noise—
slamming doors, shouted names.
Mine left like a whisper
pressed against the corners of a house
too tired to echo.

But his silence had weight.
It creaked floorboards,
waited in doorways,
and lingered in the mirror
each time I tried to see myself

whole.

Now, even grown,
I tie my shoes slowly,
like a ritual.
Not because I need to—
but because every time I do,
I forgive him
a little more.

The Voice I Borrowed

I didn't know how to speak at first,
not really.
Not with the weight I carry now.
Back then, I wore other voices
like Sunday hand-me-downs—
still starched, never mine.

My uncle's sharp edge,
my pastor's thunder,
a teacher's precise diction,
the low drawl of boys
who learned cool in the shadow of corners.
Each one a mask
I wore until it cracked.

I mimicked power
before I understood its cost.
Let syllables fall heavy,
trying to stretch my chest
to match a man's memory.

Sometimes I'd echo men on the TV—
those who moved crowds
like wind moves wheat.
Other times, I'd whisper poems
into pillows,
afraid the softness would stain me.

I was fluent in disguise

long before I spoke in truth.

But truth...
truth came like a tremble,
not a trumpet.
It sat in the back of my throat
and hummed.
Not loud—
but real.

Now, my voice stutters less,
though it still wavers when I weep.
It no longer fits into borrowed boxes.
It cracks sometimes,
and still, it is mine.
Whole in its trembling.
Unashamed in its tone.

This voice—
this slow, beautiful undoing
of every echo
I no longer need.

Hand-Me-Down Hopes

They stitched ambition into denim,
passed it down like coats
that never quite fit.
My grandfather wore hope
like a Sunday suit—creased,
clean, but tight around the shoulders.
He couldn't raise his arms too high,
but he still reached.

My mother folded her dreams
into lunch bags,
pressed them between notes in my backpack.
Sometimes I found them
creased and crumbled
between math sheets and silence.
Still warm with her handwriting.

The hopes handed to me
came with stains—
regret, struggle, sacrifice.
They whispered in the dark:
"Don't waste what we could never hold."

I tried them on
like old shoes,
walked a while in the ache of them.
Some hopes pinched,
some I wore threadbare.
Some I broke on purpose—

cracked them open
to see if anything inside was still alive.
Some I buried,
because they weren't mine
and never asked to be.

But there were a few
that fit like breath.
That smelled of soil
and hard-won joy.

So I carry them now—
not as burden,
but as blueprint.
I stitch my own hopes
with steady hands,
using thread pulled
from both rupture and reverence.

I will not pass down
what was passed down
without first
redeeming it.

Hiding Places

There was a spot behind the couch,
just wide enough for my knees
to forget they were growing.
There, I could fold the world in half—
my side quiet, theirs noisy.
I learned early how to vanish
without leaving the room.

Under the table,
between the coats in the hallway closet,
inside the scent of Pine-Sol and old sermons—
I built sanctuaries
from things nobody missed.

Sometimes, I'd crawl beneath my bed,
lie flat and still
like a secret waiting to be told.
My breath learned patience there.
My fears learned names.
I wasn't hiding from monsters.
Not the cartoon kind.
But the slam of doors.

The silence after a question.
The eyes that looked
but didn't see.

I made hiding
an art form.

Even smiled while doing it—
camouflage stitched
from good manners and quiet nods.

They said I was shy.
Said I was such a good boy.
But they never asked
why I always knew
where the shadows were softest.

Now, as a man,
I walk freely
but I still feel the corners—
spaces where I could disappear
if I needed to.

Sometimes,
I still do.

I Was There When I Wasn't

I remember the day
Grandma's hands went still—
how the room filled with flowers
that smelled nothing like her.
People kept speaking
in full, heavy sentences.
I kept answering with nods
that didn't know where to land.

They say I was there.
Say I sat in the front row,
wearing the blue suit
I hated.
Say I held Mama's hand
tight enough to leave a mark.

But I remember nothing
after the casket closed—
just the hum behind my ears,
the way light bent through stained glass
and never quite came back right.

Grief came in fragments,
like a puzzle with missing edges.
And I,
a boy too young to know

what to do with so much silence,
folded myself
into smaller and smaller corners
of thought.
I played outside later that day.
Laughed even.
Swung high on the rusted swing
as if the sky
could forget.

I was praised for being strong—
for not crying,
for "holding it together."
But truth is,
I was already somewhere else.

My body sat at the repast.
My soul,
still staring at her slippers
by the back door.

I've been trying to return to that moment
ever since—
not to relive it,
but to finally be there
as I was
meant to be.

Numb Enough to Pass

There came a time
when my laughter learned
to wait its turn—
to check the room first,
to bend itself
into something
less suspicious.

I began to speak
with softened consonants,
ironed out vowels,
a voice that folded itself
into the margin
and pretended
to belong.

They said I was "well-spoken."
Said it like a medal,
like a secret handshake
into spaces
not built for me.
I wore that praise
like a borrowed suit—
tight in the shoulders,
short at the sleeves.

At school,
I learned how to nod
at jokes not meant for me,

how to carry silence
like a briefcase
stuffed with apologies
I never owed.

And when the boys on the block
asked why I sounded
"like them,"
I shrugged,
said it was just for class.
Laughed with them
like nothing in me hurt.

I became a translator
between my skin
and their comfort.
Learned how to vanish
without leaving a room.
How to be present
without being seen.

Sometimes I wonder
who I could've been
if I never had to practice
disappearing.

But some doors
only open
for the parts of us
that play dead.

Becoming the Question

There was a morning
when I looked into the mirror
and no longer saw a boy—
only a riddle
wrapped in melanin,
framed by uncertainty,
held together by expectation.

They asked me who I was
before I knew
I could ask them the same.
Their eyes always came first—
naming me
before I had words.

Too soft.
Too Black.
Too loud when quiet.
Too still when moving.
A contradiction
they couldn't hold
without folding me into fear.

I began to carry questions
like spare change
in my pocket—
not enough to buy peace,
but enough to keep me restless.
What does it mean

to be me
without becoming
what they expect?
Without shrinking
or shouting
or becoming fluent
in disappearing?

I saw the mirror blink
once—
as if surprised
I was still looking.
As if I had the right
to hold my own gaze
and not flinch.

I didn't smile.
I didn't pose.
I didn't adjust the light.

I just stood there,
whole and undone,
and let the reflection
ask me
what took so long
to arrive.

Wounds Unspoken

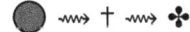

There are griefs too old for language,
and truths too dangerous to name—
but still, we carry them,
folded into our silence like survival.

⚇

Permission to Hurt

There was a moment—
just one—
where I asked myself
if it was okay
to feel the weight.

To let it settle in
like smoke beneath the ribs.
To say,
"This ache is mine."
To hold it
without apology.

They never taught me
how to bleed without shame,
only how to hide the stain.
Told me pain
was something to pray away,
or punch away,
or preach into silence.

But there are wounds
no scripture can stitch.
There are nights
when the Psalms don't speak
in the language of bruises.
Nights when even the angels
look away.

I've been the strong one
in every room—
back straight,
voice calm,
teeth clenched behind
a Sunday smile.
But strength,
like any mask,
suffocates in silence.

So today,
I give myself permission—
not to fall apart,
but to admit
I've been cracked
since childhood.

I allow the ache
to stretch out on my chest
like it paid rent.
To name the ghost
and not dress it
in metaphors.

I tell the mirror:
You are allowed to feel.
You are allowed to mourn
what never happened,
and what did.

You are allowed to say:
That hurt.
And it still does.

Because healing
is not a straight line,
and survival
is not an apology
for being broken first.

The Knock at Midnight

It is always louder than it needs to be—
even when the fist is gentle,
even when the knock is coded
with authority and assumed mistake.

Midnight knows no mercy.
It's the hour that unbuttons peace
and drapes shadows over mothers' faces.

I was not asleep—
Black boys learn early
to sleep with one ear awake.

The door trembled before we did.
My father stood without socks,
his dignity wrapped in a housecoat,
voice level, hands visible—
like a preacher calming a storm
he did not summon.

Flashlight eyes scanned
the linoleum, the baby's crib,
the family photos like mugshots
of those not yet accused.

They said wrong address.
They always say wrong address.
But fear does not return
to its drawer when corrected.

We sat in the blue hush of aftermath,
our bodies too alert to pray,
too proud to cry aloud.
And I learned—
the law can knock without cause,
and a home can bruise
without bleeding.

Unarmed, Unseen, Unforgiven

I had nothing in my hands—
not even history,
not even the anger they expected
when they saw my skin
folding sunlight into a hoodie.

Still,
the fingers on the badge
twitched like I was a lit fuse.
Still,
the stare weighed me
as a future obituary.
Still,
my breath was negotiated
in the space between
command and consequence.

I've walked through aisles
clutching nothing but silence,
yet been followed
like guilt had a scent.

I've smiled
so no one would clutch their purse,
softened my voice
so I wouldn't awaken
the ghosts of their prejudice.

But you can be dressed
in your finest self
and still be read
as an emergency.

They didn't see
my diploma
or my daughter's crayon
in my backseat.

Only potential threat.
Only walking headline.
Only what their fear
told them to see.
And that's the weight of it—
being a target
before you're a man.

A presence they practice
shooting with their stares,
rehearsing how to mourn you
without ever knowing your name.

Cuffed for Breathing

They say air is free—
but I was taxed for mine
with steel bracelets
and knees on my peace.

I wasn't marching,
wasn't shouting,
wasn't even looking them in the eye—
just breathing
like my mama taught me
when she placed my newborn chest
to hers and said,
"Inhale the world, baby.
But know it may not always
exhale you back."

And still
the street swallowed me
like I had asked for it.
Face-first.
Pulse slow-dancing
with the curb.
The pavement didn't argue—
it only held me
like a cold question
with no answer.

They cuffed me
as if I'd stolen something

other than time.
As if oxygen was contraband
and I'd smuggled it
through the color of my skin.

My only weapon was a heartbeat.
Unregistered, but present.
Pleading.

What law did I break
but the unspoken one—
that I should've disappeared
quieter?

My lungs had no protest in them,
only the rhythm of survival,
the heave of a man
trying to stay whole
in a system
that breaks you
and calls it procedure.

What the Camera Didn't Catch

The footage froze at the frame
that made the world gasp.
But there were no reels
for what came after.
No angle caught the way my spirit
slid sideways
under the weight of their hands.
No soundbite for the prayer
I mouthed to no one
because my mouth was full
of gravel and disbelief.

The camera didn't catch
how I tasted my father's fear
in that moment—
not just mine—
the way it had passed down
like a middle name.
Didn't catch
how I remembered my son
laughing that morning,
or how I wondered
if he'd inherit this silence, too.

No lens for the look they gave me—
clinical,

like I was problem,
not person.
No microphone for the insult
whispered through clenched teeth,
nor the officer's smirk
when I asked,
"What did I do?"

You saw the choke.
You saw the fall.
But you didn't see the stories
spill out of me—
the pages of dignity,
the lineage of grace,
the whole gospel of my becoming
scattered like torn paper
in the wind of their force.

They hit rewind.
They pressed play.
The world debated
what it meant.

But I lived
what they missed.

Sunday Clothes, Quiet Rage

I wore my best that morning.
Crisp collar.
Polished shoes.
A tie like restraint.
Mama said, "Dress like the Lord
might come today."
So I did.
But the Lord
didn't come.

Only questions came—
about where I was going,
about what I was doing
so clean,
so early,
so composed.
My dignity became
suspicious.

I smiled, politely.
Said "sir" with each breath
as if manners might melt
a muzzle off their eyes.
They stared through me
like Sunday was a costume
I had no right to wear.
Like I'd stolen
grace.

Their voices calm—
that careful calm
that comes before storms—
asked what I was hiding
beneath all that neat.
I said, "Just prayers."
They didn't laugh.

And when they let me go,
I didn't shout.
I didn't break.
I walked away
a cathedral of rage
with stained glass eyes,
trying not to shatter
in the daylight.

Because even in my Sunday best,
they saw
not a man
but a moment
to manage.

Crossed Legs, Clenched Fists

They told me
to soften—
to shrink the square
of my shoulders,
round off the sharpness
of my voice,
fold my power
into pleasantries.
So I crossed my legs—
a gesture
they mistook
for peace.

But beneath the table,
my fists were coiled,
holding the history
they refused to name.

There's a war in the bones
that no one sees—
because it doesn't bleed,
only burns.

I've mastered the art
of nodding when I'm not okay,
of laughing just enough
to keep from being called—
dangerous,
aggressive,

ungrateful.

They want humility
but only on their terms—
the kind that silences
without chains.

Each day,
I uncross one leg at a time
and ask myself
if I'm still a man
in this performance
of safety.

Every yes
comes with splinters
of compromise.

But one day,
these clenched fists
will rise —
not in violence,
but in truth.

And they will know—
I was never asking
for permission
to be whole.

The Silence of Being Doubted

They asked for my story
and blinked like I'd stuttered.
Paused, then nodded slow—
the kind of nod that means
we don't believe you,
but we'll pretend we might.

It's a strange kind of grief
to watch your truth
be weighed against
their comfort.

I spoke in full sentences,
offered timestamps, names,
the smell of the room,
the crack in my voice.
But their eyes
searched for holes
I hadn't left.

Being doubted
doesn't sound like shouting—
it's quieter.
A slow erasure,
like your words
are sand
and their silence
the tide.
Sometimes I speak softer

just to feel
what it's like
not to fight
for the right
to be believed.

Other times,
I stop mid-sentence
and let the hush speak
for me.
Because if my truth
must be broken
to be accepted—
I'd rather be whole
in their disbelief
than shattered
for their comfort.

A Man in a Mirror Made of Bars

There is a mirror in the cell—
not made of glass
but of metal, scratched and dull,
where a man can barely see his face,
but still sees enough
to remember who he was
before the badge-eyed men
rewrote his name.

Every day I stare into it.
Not to fix my hair—
I no longer bother—
but to ask
if I'm still there.

Behind me, the walls hum
with other forgotten names,
men who shout at ghosts,
laugh at ceilings,
or whisper their mother's hymn
into a bunk that won't listen.

I do the same sometimes.

There is no silence here—
only the sound of time

crumbling slowly
against steel.

The mirror never blinks.
It reflects me
just enough to wound—
a jaw clenched in protest,
eyes that refuse to lower,
skin branded by suspicion.

Sometimes I speak to the man in it.
Not aloud,
but in the way breath fogs steel—
a kind of communion.
He doesn't answer.
But he doesn't turn away either.

And maybe that's enough.
To know
that even behind bars,
there is a version of me
that refuses to vanish.

Black Boy, Blue Sirens

He was just learning how to ride
without hands—
how to balance joy and wind,
his laugh skipping down the street
like a stone across water.

But the sirens didn't care.

Blue lights fell on his face
like a second puberty—
a forced aging,
turning bike pedals
into suspect motives,
and skin
into a warning label.

He did what they said.
All of it.
Hands in the air,
mouth zipped like a prayer
he was too afraid to say aloud.

They asked him questions
his age hadn't grown into yet.
Where he was going.
Who he was.
Why he looked like someone
who looked like someone
who might've done something.

He tried to answer
without making waves.
But even silence
sounded like guilt
through their radios.

One wrong blink
and the wind could've stopped forever.

His mother came running.
Still in her house slippers,
shouting his name
like it was both hymn and shield.

They let him go, eventually—
told him to "be careful out here,"
as if care could stop
what color couldn't.

That night,
he didn't touch his bike.
Just sat on the steps,
watching his breath
rise and disappear—
trying to remember
the last time it felt safe
to be a boy.

The Smile They Feared

It wasn't even wide—
just a small curl
edge of sunrise
testing the sky.

A flicker of ease
where hardness
was expected,
demanded
by the world
from a face like his.

But somehow,
his smile walked into rooms
before him
and stole all the attention.
Made people grip their bags
tighter,
forget how doors work,
how nods can be returned
without suspicion.

He smiled in school
to keep the teachers calm.
Smiled in stores
to not look "interested" in stealing.
Smiled in churches
to prove
he belonged there too.

He learned to make it light—
not too bold, not too bright,
just enough to say:
"I am safe. I am not a threat.
Please let me pass."

They called it smug.
Too confident.
Too sure of himself.
Too much for someone
with nothing.

But they didn't see
how many times he practiced it
in bathroom mirrors
with cracked corners
and no applause.

Didn't know the ache
of holding up a face
that kept everyone else
comfortable
while it strangled
the boy beneath.

He smiled
to hide the tremble in his jaw,
to silence the scream
before it reached his throat.

But one day,
he let it fall.
Let the corners of his mouth
rest like tired birds.

And someone finally asked
if he was okay.
He didn't answer.
Just looked at them,
the way wounds do
when they've run out of
ways to be seen.

I Am Not Your Apology

Don't hand me the bouquet
of your regret.
Don't drape your sorrys
like a medal over my silence
and expect me to wear it
with pride.

I am not your closure.
Not the page you dog-eared
in a book you never finished
but quote at parties.

You look at me
with eyes full of lessons
I never asked to teach.
Hold up my skin
like a mirror to your progress
and say,
"See how far we've come?"

But I remember
when my pain
was just background noise
to your comfort.
When my bruises
were theories you debated
instead of truths you believed.

Now, you want to sit across from me
with trembling lips and trembling hands
and tell me how sorry you are.

But you are not owed my healing
as evidence of your change.
You are not entitled to my forgiveness
as proof that you've evolved.

I will not be the black backdrop
against which your white redemption
shines brighter.

I am not the smile
at the end of your documentary,
the handshake after your seminar,
the anecdote you use
to calm a guilty room.

If you must apologize—
do it to the mirror.
To your children.
To the system you benefit from
in silence.

But don't make me
your reckoning.
Don't turn my survival
into your salvation.

I am not your apology.
I am the reason you needed one.

The Language of Less Than

They spoke in measurements—
not inches,
not pounds,
but silence.

A nod too slow,
a handshake too firm,
a pause before the word sir,
like they were checking
if I deserved it.

In rooms where worth
was a whisper
measured by collars stiffened
and voices lowered,
I entered fluent
in a dialect
I was never taught—
the language of less than.

It lives in the shift of eyes
when I speak too boldly,
in the sudden stillness
when I mention
the fullness of my dreams.
In how I am corrected
even when I am right.
In how I am told
how well I speak

for a man like me.

I've learned to speak in echoes—
words softened,
thoughts trimmed,
ambition laced
with apology.
I code my voice
in nonthreatening tones,
my truths
in careful metaphors.

Because to speak plainly
is to be too loud.
To stand firmly
is to be too proud.
To feel fully
is to be too much.

I was taught to barter
my brilliance
for their comfort.
To translate my value
into their currency.
To erase my grammar
to match their sentences.

But I am tired
of speaking less,
to be heard more.
Tired of folding myself
into the shape
of their acceptance.

So now,

I write in my own tongue.
Unedited.
Unapologetic.
Untranslated.

Because I am not less.
Never was.

And this voice—
this full, cracked, rising voice—
was never theirs to measure.

In My Shadow

Some days,
I walk outside
and feel a second sun
trailing behind me—
not light,
but heat.
The heat of being watched
just enough
to sweat.

I've never been to Mississippi.
Never touched
the muddy hush of a riverbank
where innocence drowned
beneath the weight of being seen,
of being heard,
of simply being.
But I carry the echo—
like breath I didn't ask for,
like a shadow
I dare not forget.

They tell us
times have changed.
But my mother still flinches
when I wear a hoodie at night.
Still texts twice
if she hears sirens
before I answer.

I am not him,
but I've seen his echo
in the rearview mirror
when a cruiser slows down.
I've heard him
in the tight voice
of a teacher
explaining my "attitude."
Felt him
in the rustle of purses clutched
in elevators.
He is in every glance
that asks
what I'm doing here.

Some ghosts don't haunt—
they inherit.
They pass themselves
from breath to breath,
from boy to man
to boy again.
And we carry them,
not in fear,
but in warning.

Not in mourning,
but in memory.

I see him
not just in museums
or black-and-white stills—
I see him in reflections
that twitch
when I smile.

In the nervous chuckles
of people
who say they don't see color,
but still cross the street.

He walks with me
on sidewalks
my tax dollars paved,
into stores
my money funds,
through neighborhoods
my peace
has yet to buy.

He is the shadow
that reminds me
this world
was built to fear
the shape
of my joy.

And still,
I walk.
I speak.
I laugh louder
than they'd like.
Because he
deserves more
than silence.
And I—
I deserve
to live.

The Womb I Never Knew

They say I was born
like every other child—
wet with want,
lungs learning how to wail,
cradled in cotton
and questions.

But I have always wondered
about the space
I never came from.
The warmth
that didn't hold me.
The heartbeat
I never listened to
from the inside.

Was there a voice
meant to name me
softer?
Hands
that might have traced
my face with reverence
instead of regret?

I search crowds
for a chin like mine,
a brow that breaks
the same way
when I worry.

Even as a man,
I ache
like an orphaned dream
for something
I've never touched.

They say wombs are sacred—
but what of the one
that let me go?
Am I still holy
without it?

Sometimes,
I wonder if the world
feels colder
because I never had
that first fire—
that unspoken
belonging
to someone
who would have called me
"son"
before I ever earned it.

I have met mothers
who hum when they hug.
Mothers who can read
their children's silences.
Mothers who
build safety
with a glance.

And I—
I have learned
to mother myself

in parking lots,
in prison cells,
in barber chairs
and cracked mirrors.
To bandage my fears
with borrowed grace.
To lullaby myself
to sleep
in the arms of God.

The womb I never knew
taught me
a quiet resilience—
to become
what was missing,
to love
like I was never left,
to live
as if my very breath
was a protest
against being forgotten.

And maybe,
just maybe—
that
is a birthright
too.

Indicted By Hue

There are courts
that never call themselves such—
sidewalks
where judgments fall
without gavels,
store aisles
where suspicion follows
like a second shadow,
school desks
where my name
is mispronounced
but my body
is already understood.

This skin—
this brown-lit burden—
is the only evidence
they ever need.

I've stood
in the lineup of stares,
been read
my rights to remain silent
before I even spoke,
felt verdicts settle
in the curl of their lips
when I enter a room
with my head high.
I was tried

the day I was born.
Tried for being loud
without speaking,
dangerous
without doing,
angry
without anger.

Every breath
in public
is cross-examined.
Every stride
on a quiet street
is a closing argument
against my innocence.

Sometimes I wonder
if God weeps
watching His image
feared
in a hoodie.
If angels clench
their golden fists
when we are sentenced
to suspicion
for the crime
of walking home.

I know how to say
"yes, officer"
like a liturgy.
I've mastered
the hush
that might save my life.
I've learned

how to lower
my humanity
just enough
to be seen
as safe.

But I ask you—
what justice lives
in a world
where skin
can be cross-examined
before character?
Where the scales of justice
tilt at the weight
of melanin?

And still,
we rise.
With dignity unsentenced,
with laughter unjailed,
with songs that break
every cell's silence.

Because we are more
than the trials we carry—
we are testimony,
we are truth,
and we are tired
of being
the accused
in a world
we helped build.

My Name, Their Weapon

They ask it first—
like a riddle
they've already solved.
"What's your name?"
But not to know me.
To size me.
To sheath suspicion
in syllables.

My name is not strange.
It is scripture.
It is legacy.
It is the hum
of generations
who refused
to be renamed.

But when they hear it,
their brows raise
like I've confessed
to something.
Like I've already done
too much
by just being
named.

They mispronounce it
with purpose,
twisting it

until it limps,
mocking the music
my mother whispered
into my birth.

Some say it's too long—
as if my identity
should be shortened
for their comfort.
Others say it's "ghetto"—
as if home
is something shameful
in the mouth.

But the worst
are those
who use it
like a slur—
like a warning
to others.
"Watch him."
They don't say it out loud,
but it echoes
in the hallways,
in the pauses,
in the eyes
that linger
a second too long.

My name
has been called
in courtrooms
where I stood
as both witness
and accused.

It has been shouted
by teachers
who never asked
how to say it right.
It has been printed
in reports
that reduced me
to incident.

But still,
my name stands.
Not just as a title—
but a resistance.
A reminder.
A melody
that survived
ships, chains,
and silences.

So I say it
with pride.
Spell it slow
if you must.
But know this—
my name
is not your weapon.
It is my shield.
It is my story.
And every time
you try to twist it,
you only prove
why it must never
be changed.

The Fragile Hallelujah of Black Love

They only see the headlines—
not the holding on.
Not the hands
gripping each other
like ropes in a storm.
Not the silent "I'm here"
echoed in the squeeze
before the door shuts.

They do not see
how we laugh
with tired lungs.
How joy dances
even in a war zone—
not because it's easy,
but because it's ours.

Black love—
not the kind in movies,
but the kind
that learns to love
through police lights,
through death scrolling by
on phones,
through history
that won't stay

in the past tense.
It's midnight prayers
over brown sons
and fragile futures.
It's "text me when you get home"
and the deep breath
after the text comes.

It's building a home
in a world
that keeps trying
to burn it down.
It's not perfection—
it's survival
with tenderness.

Black love
has been called
too loud,
too angry,
too much.
But maybe
that's what makes it holy—
that it keeps blooming
despite being buried
beneath centuries
of don't, can't, won't.

But with love
comes pain—
not because we fail,
but because we fight.
We fight to be seen,
to be soft,
to be whole

in a country
that edits us
out of its dream.
Sometimes,
we hurt each other—
not because we want to,
but because we've been taught
that love
is another battlefield.
We unlearn the lies
one hug at a time.

Black love,
Black pain—
two sides
of the same scar.
But even scars
are proof
that something healed.

When Brothers Betray

He looked like me—
walked like me,
called me "brother"
with the same tongue
that would twist the knife.

We shared the same streets,
same chalk-line threats,
same nods at the corner store
when eyes said, I got you.
But somewhere
between survival
and self-preservation,
he forgot the code.

It wasn't the betrayal
that shattered me—
it was the memory
of laughing with the hand
that would later
leave me bleeding.

There's a different kind of wound
when your own reflection
strikes you.
When the face you trusted
sells you for nothing
but fear dressed in silence.
How many times

have I stood
on trial in his mouth?
He called it truth,
but it was just
his way of hiding
the mirror.

I've seen brothers
turn each other in
just to feel
less hunted.
As if feeding me
to the system
would buy them
a freer night's sleep.

But it doesn't.
It just breaks us
into smaller pieces—
sharp enough
to stab each other
before the world even has to.
Still—
I mourn him.
Not because I miss him,
but because I miss
what we could've been
had we held each other
instead of loading
our pain
into accusations.

They say brotherhood is blood.
But sometimes,
it's betrayal

that makes you see
who was only
playing kin.

And yet...
I forgive him.
Not because he asked.
Not because he earned it.
But because I refuse
to let his shadow
take my light.

This Ain't My Cross—But I Carry It

They handed it to me
without words—
just looks,
just laws,
just the long silence
between a question
and the assumption
that I was guilty.

I didn't build this burden.
Didn't hammer the shame,
didn't carve the blame,
didn't draw the line
that said You there, suffer.
But I carry it
like it's my inheritance.

Every step I take
with this invisible weight
pulls me lower—
but they only see me
bowed
and call it submission.

They say,
Why are you always angry?

I say,
Why am I always bleeding?

My name,
my skin,
my stride,
all filed under suspicion—
a man crucified
on the post of perception.

Still, I wake.
Still, I walk.
Still, I pray
with back bent
and breath borrowed
from dreams I'm still owed.

This ain't my cross—
but I carry it.
Because someone has to show
what dignity looks like
when it's cracked
but not crushed.

Someone has to sing
while nailed to history.
Someone has to speak
while choked by silence.
Someone has to live
so others can breathe
one breath
less burdened.
I carry it.
Not because I choose to,
but because

I refuse
to let it bury me
without making
the dirt remember
my name.

Tears and Thunder

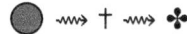

I have heard God in broken rhythms,
in thunder without rain,
in the voices of ancestors
who taught me to speak
even while trembling.

I Dream in Fire

Some nights
the flames speak my name
in a tongue older than the wound,
older than the lash,
older than the first time I was told to bow
before something that did not make me holy.

My dreams do not burn houses—
they burn silence.
They ignite the hush passed down
like bad inheritance—
generational quiet
tucked beneath every Sunday suit
and forced smile.

I am not running from fire.
I am walking through it—
barefoot and deliberate,
each step a sermon
my father never dared preach
but whispered
in the crackle of his knuckles
each time the world made him kneel
without cause.

In these dreams,
I wear ash like anointing oil.
Smoke wraps my shoulders
like the arms of ancestors

chanting,
"Burn, child, not in anger—
but in becoming."

And I awaken
not afraid of the fire
but afraid
of forgetting
that I was forged in it.

Psalms from My Bones

I do not read scripture
from pages anymore.
The gospel echoes
in the aching of my knees,
in the marrow where grief settles
like a stubborn hymn.

There are verses etched
along my collarbone—
words I never learned in church
but felt
when silence broke my back
and left me breathing through prayer
I didn't know I was speaking.

My bones have learned
how to carry sorrow
like communion.
Each ache, a hallelujah.
Each crack, a testimony.

This is how I worship now:
not with folded hands,
but clenched fists raised
toward a sky that forgot
how to answer softly.

Some psalms scream.
Some weep.

Some do both
in the space between ribs
where I still believe
God is listening,
even when He stays quiet.

And if no choir sings my song,
so be it—
the echo will live
in the places that hurt,
in the places still healing,
in the sacred tremble
of a man who dares
to still believe.

The Storm Inside My Father's Voice

It wasn't thunder
that first taught me fear—
it was the way my father's voice cracked
when he told me
life would not love me back.

There was rain
in the way he paused,
as if each word weighed too much
for his breath to carry.
A drizzle of disappointment
coated every syllable.

When he raised his voice,
the windows in my chest shook.
But even in his quiet,
I heard a storm
gathering behind his teeth—
not rage,
but grief
with nowhere to go.

His voice was the sound
of a man who once dreamed
and buried every dream
beneath bills,

betrayals,
and nights spent preaching
to a God
who sometimes felt
too white
to understand him.

I learned to listen
not for what he said,
but for what trembled underneath:
regret wrapped in resolve,
a warning disguised as love.

And still—
on certain nights
when the wind sighs low
through the trees,
I swear I hear it again:
his voice
not breaking,
but bending—
like a branch refusing
to fall.

When the Dead Speak Through Wind

It was never just wind
through the branches—
it was whisper.
It was witness.
It was the weary breath
of those who walked before me
and never got to run.

I stood still once,
beneath a tree older than
this country's memory,
and the air shifted
like a sermon—
soft, sorrowful,
stern.

They spoke not in words
but in rustle,
in hush,
in the sacred shiver
of skin that remembers
what the mind forgets.

My great-grandmother's hum,
my uncle's unfinished sentence,
the moan of a man

whose name they didn't carve
into history—
they all passed through me
like smoke
that knew my name.

The wind doesn't lie.
It carries every hallelujah
that cracked from a throat
caged in chain.
Every lullaby
rocked in cotton fields
and bloodied cradles.
Every breath stilled
before it could testify.

So I listen.
When the breeze leans in,
I open the doors
of my body
like a chapel
without walls.

And I answer,
with trembling yes,
to voices
I never met
but somehow
always knew.

Thunder Without Rain

There are nights
when the sky growls
like it remembers
every injustice
ever buried beneath silence.

Thunder rolls
not as promise,
but as protest—
a deep, aching roar
with no mercy
in its echo.

No rain follows.
Just the sound
of something holy
restraining its hand.

And I know that feeling—
the weight of eruption
held in the chest,
the crackling edge
of breaking
that never breaks.

I've walked with storms
in my ribcage,
shouted into pillows
like clouds that could not burst.

Trembled with fury
that had no exit,
no sky
to fall into.

They called me composed,
calm,
"well-spoken"—
but I was thunder
swallowed.
Lightning
chained to silence.

You learn,
after a while,
to live as warning.
To carry noise
like a prophecy,
to speak only
when your voice
can rattle stone.

Because sometimes,
thunder is all
we're allowed.
No rain.
Just the sound
of what might have healed
if they had only
listened.

Spirits in the Cotton

They never left.
Not the ones who bent like stalks
under sun-thick air,
who sang hymns with dirt in their teeth
and hope in cracked palms.
I walk past fields
where cotton still blooms like ghosts,
soft and white
as if innocence could grow
from blood.
But I've heard the hum—
low like mourning,
rising like prayer—
when wind combs the rows
as if fingers still reach
for something more
than harvest.

My grandfather said,
"The land remembers."
And I believe it—
the way my spine straightens
on soil that once swallowed
our stories whole.

Every tuft whispers
the names
they wouldn't carve into stone.
Every bloom

is a soul they couldn't break.

I saw one once—
a glimmer by the cotton gin,
eyes full of dust and deliverance.
He nodded at me
like we shared
the same scar.

The children don't play there.
Even they feel
the hush in the roots,
the ache in the bloom.

It is sacred.
It is haunted.
It is ours.

I Prayed in a Language I Never Learned

It wasn't English
or tongues
or anything taught in pews
with padded seats
and air conditioning.

It came raw—
a cry shaped like thunder
but softer than breath.
A sound I didn't know I knew
until it left me
as if remembering
was a form of release.

My lips parted,
and something older than voice
poured out,
filling the room with syllables
that tasted like clay,
salt,
and longing.

I didn't understand them,
but I trusted them.
Because my bones
leaned forward to listen

and the silence afterward
felt holy.

Maybe it was my ancestors
speaking through me,
using my body
like a reed,
a riverbed,
a drum.
Maybe grief taught me
how to talk to God
in a dialect
grief had to invent.

Or maybe
some prayers don't need translation
because ache
is a universal tongue
and heaven
ain't that far from the wound.

Shackles in the Soul

I walk free,
but something clinks
when I move too quickly
toward joy.

Invisible iron
tightens when I laugh too loud,
love too hard,
hope too much.

It is the weight
of lessons never meant to be mine—
to be still,
to be strong,
to be silent,
to survive.

Passed down like heirlooms
with no receipt,
these restraints came wrapped
in "be a man,"
"don't cry,"
"don't scare them."

I tried unlocking them
with education,
religion,
resistance,
but still they rattle

in my chest
when I'm alone with the truth.

The truth is:
freedom isn't just not being owned.
It's being known
without having to perform
your humanity.

It's resting
without guilt,
weeping
without shame,
being Black
without armor.

I want to walk
and hear nothing but breath.
No chains.
No echo of fear.
Just the holy silence
of a soul finally unshackled.

The Prophet in Me Trembled

I didn't ask
to see
what others
refuse to name.
Didn't want this gift
that cuts
like a curse—
vision too clear
for comfort,
truth too sharp
for silence.

The prophet in me
does not wear robes.
He wears calloused hands,
a trembling jaw,
and eyes that've watched
too many futures burn
before they bloomed.
He rose in me one night
while I was praying for peace,
and said—

"First, you must disturb the dust."
So I spoke.
And they called it anger.
I wept.
And they called it weakness.

I stood still.
And they called it defiance.

But I know what I heard
when Spirit cracked the stillness—
that I was made to unsettle,
to sing before the storm,
to cry into the hollow places
and make them echo
with the memory of justice.

Yet still—
the prophet in me trembled.
Not from doubt,
but from the ache
of knowing
that even truth
has a cost.
And sometimes—
the bearer bleeds.

Dust of the Ancestors

They said the land was barren,
but I knelt
and felt it breathe.
Not empty—
just filled with memory.
Ash of the burned,
bone of the burdened,
sweat salted into soil
by hands that were never paid
but always praying.

When the wind kicks up,
I don't just see dust—
I see names
dancing in the light,
shadows of those
who dared to walk
even when chains clanged
like thunder behind them.

I've heard them in cotton fields,
in church pews that creak with history,
in hymns hummed low
when language was a whip
and silence was survival.

They are not gone.
They are ground
beneath every step I take,

rising in my breath,
settling in my blood.

I carry them
like a spine,
like the rhythm of my walk,
like the hush
before I speak truth
they never had the chance to say.

Their dust
is not decay—
it is declaration.

Holy Rage

They told me anger was sin,
but I watched Jesus flip tables
and knew holiness could roar.

This rage
is not reckless—
it is sacred fire.
A burning bush
in my belly
that will not be consumed
until justice
is more than a sermon.

My rage knows scripture,
can quote pain
like gospel:
"In the beginning was the wound,
and the wound was with us,
and the wound was us."

I have prayed
through clenched teeth,
fasted on silence,
tithing my dignity
to pews that asked me
to smile through chains.

But today,
I wear my anger like a robe,

a prophet's garment
woven from centuries of grief.
And still—
I do not curse.
I construct.
I do not burn bridges.
I build altars
in the ashes.

Holy is the rage
that refuses to forget.
Holy is the rage
that still hopes.
Holy is the rage
that breaks
only to bloom again.

Sermons From My Shadow

I did not know I was preaching
until I heard my silence echo
in the ears of men
who feared what I had not said.

My shadow testifies.
It steps into rooms before me,
gathers assumptions,
pulls whispers into pews
where none of us
ever asked to sit.

There are sermons in how I stand.
In how I carry
the burden of being seen
as threat
and savior
in the same glance.

There's a gospel
in the crack of my spine
where oppression hunched me
but never bowed me.
Where grief stretched itself into psalms
I sang with no melody—
only memory.

Even in stillness,
my shadow teaches:

how to walk without apology,
how to dance in steel-toed silence,
how to turn a curse
into communion.

I have buried too many brothers
to not speak
when the air trembles
with injustice.
So I let my silhouette speak
what my mouth can't—
its dark shape a scripture
on the walls of history,
spelling freedom
one footstep at a time.

Drums Beneath My Skin

There are drums beneath my skin—
not for music,
but memory.

They beat
when the world forgets
how we got here.
When names are lost
to soil,
to silence,
to systems
that still pretend
they don't know our sound.

In my chest,
the rhythm returns:
grandfather's hands,
mother's prayers,
the breath between no and survive.
Each thump
a footfall on a path
paved with ash and hallelujahs.

Some days, I walk to the beat
of a war I never started
but was born into.
Other days,
the drums slow,
soft as a lullaby

sung by those
who didn't make it home
but made a way anyway.

I do not play them.
They play me—
guiding my steps
like the tide follows the moon.
Like grief finds its way
back to the body.

They are ancient,
these drums,
and sacred.
They carry no lies,
only lineage.

So when I speak,
know this:
my voice is just a vessel.
What you're hearing
is the echo of those
who still hum
through the hollow
of my bones.

Every Scar Is Scripture

This body is not broken—
it is annotated.
Each scar, a psalm
written in the ink of survival,
a gospel
etched in the aftermath
of almost.

Do not ask me to hide them.
Do not ask me
what I did to deserve them.
Ask instead
what I had to become
to live beyond their making.

There is theology
in torn skin—
a sermon in the split lip,
a hymn in the spine's slow bend
beneath burdens unnamed.
And the flesh remembers
what tongues forgot.

I trace the wound on my wrist
like a scholar of sacred things—
it speaks of silence broken,
of the day I chose to stay,
of the hour I heard God
in my own breath.

You want proof
of the divine?
Look no further
than the healed places—
those ragged, radiant altars
where pain once prayed
for peace.

And still, I rise
like scripture resurrected.
Not flawless—
but faithful.
Not spotless—
but seen.

So when I say I know God,
know this:
it is because I have bled,
and was not abandoned.

The Sky Told Me to Rise

I laid in fields of doubt
with my back to the breath of God,
asking the soil
why it always welcomed me
like a coffin.

But the sky—
it whispered louder than despair,
poured blue into my bones,
stretched light across my chest
like a second chance.

"Rise," it said,
not as command,
but invitation.
As if it remembered
the boy I buried in myself
and wanted him back.

My knees cracked like old hymns.
I stood
on promises I forgot I made—
to my mother,
to the mirror,
to the man I swore I'd become.

I carried clouds on my shoulders,
thunder in my belly,
a sunlit bruise of hope

across my spine.

They thought I was down,
but gravity never owned me.
I had wings
made of sighs and surrender,
stitched together
in midnights I didn't think
I'd live through.

So if you see me now,
standing still but lifted—
know the sky
once bent low to meet me,
and told me I was not done.

Baptized in Grief

I was not dipped in water,
but in absence—
in the slow, unholy ache
of goodbye
before the lips could form it.

Grief touched my forehead
like oil from a trembling hand,
marking me chosen
by sorrow too ancient for language.

No choir sang.
Only the wind,
moaning low
through the ribs of a house
where joy used to live.

I knelt on the floor of memory,
drenched in echoes—
my own cries
folding into the moan
of every man who'd lost
without permission.

There is a river that runs
beneath the skin of Black men—
a current made of losses
we carry in silence,
like smuggled thunder.

In that water,
I did not wash clean.
I remembered.
I became—

not free,
but full—
of the weight
that made my back a mountain.

And when I rose,
grief did not leave me.
It stood beside me,
still dripping,
whispering,
"Now you understand."

Songs My Grandfather Left Behind

He never wrote them down.
Didn't need to.
They lived in his humming—
low, earth-deep,
like a tractor engine warming
before sunrise.

Each note held
the patience of cracked hands,
the hush between field rows,
the holler of a people
too proud to die quietly.

He sang with no audience
but sky and stubborn soil,
his voice carrying
into the ribs of trees,
into my bones
before I even knew
they could carry melody.

I didn't understand the words—
if there were any.
Just the weight of them,
the way they pulled
against silence

like a mule against bridle.
Now, I hum without knowing why.
In the mirror,
his jawline rides my face
like a familiar tune.
His rhythm walks in my stride.
His breath
waits in the spaces
between my prayers.

There is a song I can't forget—
because I never learned it.
Because it was already
waiting inside me
the day I was born.

God, Are You Listening to Black Men?

We don't pray like the pictures
in children's Bibles—
knees clean, hands folded,
eyes soft like lambs.
We pray with cracked voices,
callused hands,
and tongues swollen
from too many swallowed words.

We don't whisper our suffering.
We shout it in silence.
Our pain is not quiet—
it is coded.
In the tilt of the chin.
The way we watch the door.
The tension behind a smile
meant to ease suspicion.

We cry out beneath breath,
because breath
gets taken from us.

We are told You listen.
That You know
when sparrows fall.
But do You hear

when a man
pretends not to be breaking?

Do You notice
when our praise comes
with clenched fists,
when our hallelujahs
limp through memories
of cell blocks,
betrayals,
and mothers we couldn't save?

If You listen—
can You also answer
in a voice that doesn't sound
like waiting?

Let it thunder in our marrow,
split the heavens
if You must.
But please—
say something
we can feel
before our sons
forget how to ask.

The River Knows My Name

Before I ever learned
to spell redemption,
I heard it
in the hush of a riverbend,
where water carried
secrets older than sorrow.

The river does not forget.
It remembers the weight
of chained ankles,
the lullabies of escape,
the trembling of freedom
whispered through reeds
at midnight.
When I knelt beside it,
I did not speak—
I listened.

It knew the taste
of my grandfather's grief.
It carved my father's silence
into its banks.
It knew me
before I was ready
to be known.

This river—
it baptizes without asking
for permission.

It calls each name
the way a mother might
call her son home
after war.

I gave it my questions.
It gave me its flow.
We exchanged burdens
like old friends
meeting again
at the edge
of brokenness.

And when I left,
wet with the truth
of my own becoming,
I swore—
if no one else would remember me,
the river would.

I Bled, Therefore I Believed

I did not find God in stained glass,
but in the iron scent of my own blood—
when the world split my name
and I held the pieces
like a broken hymn.

Faith was never a gentle thing.
It was the groan between bruises,
the yes behind clenched teeth,
the breath that refused
to be stolen.

I bled on sidewalks,
on pulpits,
in bedrooms too quiet
after betrayal.
I bled while smiling,
while preaching,
while being strong
for everyone
but myself.

Each drop
was a scripture
they never taught me—
a psalm without melody,
a gospel of survival.

I believed

because bleeding was proof
I had not been silenced.
Because even pain,
when named,
becomes a prayer.

And when I looked at my wounds,
I saw the fingerprints
of every ancestor
who refused to die quietly.

This belief—
it is not neat.
It is not clean.
It is holy
because it lived
through the hemorrhage.

To Be a Father, To Be a Man

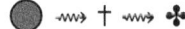

I was not handed a blueprint—
only questions,
scars,
and the aching hope
that I could build something softer
than what built me.

Teaching My Son to Walk Upright

I do not teach him to march—
not in single-file obedience
or under the gaze of fear
that polices his joy before it forms.

I teach him to walk—
not just with feet,
but with the memory in his bones
of ancestors who danced through chains
and still knew rhythm.

I teach him to walk
shoulders uncurled from shame,
eyes not hunting for danger
but naming the sky.

I show him that upright
does not mean unbent by grief—
it means rising through it,
wearing truth without flinching.

When we pass men who look away
or cross the street at our brown skin,
I do not rush him.
I let him feel the weight,
then walk through it anyway.

He asks me once if walking upright
will make him a target.
I kneel and tell him—
it may.

But so will kneeling.
So will crawling.
So will silence.

And so we walk.
Not with arrogance,
but with the dignity
no history could beat out of us.

He walks behind me now—
but not for long.
One day he will lead,
and my prayers will follow
like shadows that bless,
not burden.

The Tools My Father Left

He left behind
a rusted toolbox
half-filled with wrenches
and whole silences.

No manual,
no blueprint
for how to hold a crying child
without trembling.

But I remember—
the way he'd fix things
without speaking,
his hands a language
I am still trying to translate.

A hammer,
its handle smooth from years
of gripping what the world would not bend.
A level,
always off by just enough
to teach me how to measure imperfection with grace.
A screwdriver,
flat-headed and worn down,
like the patience it took
to raise me without raising his voice
unless he had to.

He left his tools in the garage

and his tools in my spirit—
persistence,
stillness,
grit not sharpened by anger
but carved by restraint.

He didn't tell me
how to father,
how to love,
how to break without making a sound.
But I hear him
each time I reach for a tool
and something inside me tightens
before I begin.

He left just enough—
not to build the world,
but to start again
where he stopped.

My Daughter, My Revolution

She entered the world
not quietly,
but as thunder interrupting still skies—
her cry louder
than centuries of silencing.
They told me
to raise her gently.
I chose instead
to raise her awake.

Each morning,
I watch her braid resistance
into her hair.
Each question she asks
breaks the spine
of old hierarchies.

She does not walk—
she marches.
Every step a protest
against shrinking herself
to fit someone else's comfort.

She plays with dolls
and revolution in the same afternoon.
And when she hugs me,

it is not weakness—
it is strategy.

I tell her bedtime stories
that begin with chains
and end with crowns.
She listens with eyes
like lit fuses,
knowing she was born
not to be saved,
but to save.

I do not fear for her future.
I fear for the world
that still hasn't learned
how to kneel
before the holiness
of a Black girl
unapologetically rising.

She is my daughter.
She is my revolution.
And every time she calls me Daddy,
I prepare the world
for its reckoning.

Prayers Before Bedtime Battles

Lord,
tonight he would not sleep.
His fists were full of protest,
his voice—too young to curse—
still somehow cursed the night
with questions I couldn't answer.

He said the shadows move
even when the lights are off,
and I didn't have the theology
to disprove him.

So I knelt,
beside his bed,
beside his fear,
beside the toy soldier
he broke today
because war looked too much
like his own home.

Father of restless sons,
teach me to cradle
his fury
without extinguishing his fire.
Let my hands be firm enough
to hold the storm,

but soft enough
to teach him calm.

He asked me
if angels look like him—
brown skin,
braided hair,
battle in the bones.
I told him
angels don't need wings
when they have purpose.

Tonight,
I offered no lullabies.
Only truth,
and a quiet promise
to meet him
again in the morning,
still trying,
still believing,
still praying
even if sleep never comes.

The Hands That Held Nothing

My father came home
with pockets full of echoes—
not change,
not bread,
not keys to promise,
just the weight
of everything he couldn't give.

He held me
like someone trying to remember
how to hold a dream
without breaking it.

His hands knew labor,
but not always love.
They built roofs over our silence,
fixed sinks that kept dripping doubt,
but they never quite learned
how to say "I'm proud of you"
without a shadow
in the room.

Still,
those hands,
calloused by survival,
were never closed in rage.

Even when they shook
from unpaid bills
and unspoken fears,
they reached for me—
tender in their trembling.

He never owned a Bible,
but he laid down sacrifice
like scripture.

I learned
that sometimes a man gives all
without ever having much.
And that's a holy kind of offering
the world rarely sees—
the blessing
of empty hands
that still stay open.

Blueprints for a Manhood Rebuilt

They handed me manhood
like a crumpled map
to a city that no longer exists—
roads cracked,
signs missing,
directions scrawled in pride and pain.

Be tough.
Don't cry.
Win.
Provide.
Hide the ache behind your chest
like it's contraband.

But I was born
in the aftershock of that silence—
raised on love
that didn't always know
how to name itself.
So I gathered pieces
from voices the world tried to hush.

I rebuilt manhood
from my mother's resilience,
my brother's forgiveness,
my own grief made sacred.

I drew strength from softness,
wore vulnerability like armor,
learned to speak without raising my fists.
I bent,
but did not break.
And when I did break—
I bled truth,
not shame.

This blueprint?
It's not made of steel.
It's made of skin,
spirit,
and songs
passed down
in tears.

Here,
a man can cradle hope
without crushing it.
Here,
he is allowed to be whole.

When the Boy Looks Back

He stands in the shadow
of the man I've become,
eyes wide with questions
I never answered—
or couldn't.

He asks
why the world kept calling him weak
for holding too tightly
to his mother's hand,
why tears tasted like betrayal,
why silence became
his only fluent language.

He remembers
the Sunday shoes that didn't fit,
the voice that cracked
under the weight of trying to be
someone else's definition
of strong.

I look at him now
and I don't know
if I want to apologize
or thank him—
for surviving me.

For swallowing the things
I wasn't ready to feel,

for believing in mornings
even when night
wrapped itself around his bed
like a secret.

He never blamed me,
only waited—
waited for the man to turn,
to speak,
to notice
the boy had always been there.
Watching.
Hoping.
Needing not perfection—
just presence.

And so I bend to him,
not as his future
but as his companion.
We walk together now,
side by side—
man and memory—
no longer afraid
of what we see
when we look back.

A Man of Sunday and Saturday

On Sunday, I am clean.
Pressed shirt, polished shoes,
a Bible tucked under arm
like it holds all my answers.

I shake hands with grace,
nod with humility,
sing hymns with a voice
I save for sacred things.
The congregation sees
a man carved from prayer—
upright, unshaken.

But Saturday knows me differently.
The dust under my fingernails,
the engine grease in my laugh,
the cursing that leaks when a wrench slips—
this is worship too.
In a different tongue.

My children see both—
one man in two lights.
The one who kneels to pray
and the one who kneels to fix
a leaky faucet
or broken toy

or trembling heart.

Some say you must choose.
But I believe in the middle ground—
where faith meets flesh,
where holy is not hidden
in stained glass
but revealed in tired eyes
that still keep watch

over doorframes and dreams.
I am both.
Sweat and sacrament.
Work boots and communion.
A man of Sunday and Saturday.
Because my family needs
more than a sermon—
they need a life lived
in both prayer
and presence.

The Silence Between My Father's Words

He wasn't a man of many sentences.
He spoke in nods, in worn-out sighs,
in the way he folded his hands
when thinking too hard
about bills or broken things.

What he didn't say—
that's what raised me.

The silence before he answered
was a long hallway
I had to walk alone.
No explanations for the way
he clenched his jaw
when the news mentioned justice,
or why he stared at his plate
a little longer
after Sunday dinner.

When I asked if he was proud,
he just patted my shoulder
twice.
That was his "yes."
That was his thunder.

His words were brief—

but his pauses spoke books.
They said:
I love you but can't say it
the way you need.
I've been hurt too long to risk
sounding soft.
The world already cuts deep—
I need to be stone
so you don't shatter.

Now I listen for silence
like some men search for answers.
In the hush between my own sentences,
I hear him still.
His truth not in what he said,
but in what he carried
quietly—
so I wouldn't have to.

Legacy in the Lullaby

I hum the song my mother sang
when the world weighed her eyes shut,
a tune passed down
without sheet music
but stitched in breath.

My daughter curls in the bend of my arm—
small as a promise,
wild as a question I don't yet know how to answer.
And I hum.
Because words might fail,
but melody remembers.

The lullaby isn't just a song—
it's a map.
A way through shadows,
a rhythm older than pain.
It holds the hands of ancestors
who sang through slavery,
who whispered over the cries of newborns
in cabins made of sorrow and survival.

Tonight, the tune holds my fear like a cradle.
Will she be safe?
Will this world give her room to bloom
without trimming her brilliance
to make her palatable?

I sing anyway.

Not to erase the dark—
but to show her
the sound of light fighting through it.

Each note is a thread in a tapestry
of fathers trying,
failing,
rising again.
Trying again.

She yawns,
not knowing she sleeps
on centuries of lullabies
braided into a father's breath.
Tonight, the tune holds my fear like a cradle—
rocking me too,
telling me I am not the first man
to wonder if love is enough
to build a future out of fragments.

My daughter shifts,
sighs a sound that might be peace.
And in that moment,
I believe a song can save us.

Not from the world,
but from forgetting
we were born
with music in our marrow,
and the right to sing
softness into survival.

So I hum.
Even when my voice trembles.
Because she will remember

how it felt
to be held by a lullaby
that knew her name
before she spoke it.

Man Enough to Cry

The first time it happened,
I was alone.
Tears came like unwelcome visitors—
no warning, no knocking—
just the ache breaking open
what I'd been taught to seal shut.

I remembered my father's face,
stoic as stone,
even at funerals,
even when I left.
A lesson in how to hold pain
like a secret
buried with the dead.

But what if manhood
isn't in the holding back,
but in the letting go?
What if every tear
is a baptism,
a washing away
of lies that said
we must be hard to survive?

Tonight, I cried beside my son—
not from grief,
but from the beauty of him sleeping,
the quiet rise and fall of his breath,
steady as forgiveness,

like a psalm I didn't know I needed.

One small hand curled beneath his cheek,
and all my armor fell away.
From the unbearable softness
that love demands
without apology,
I did not hide it.

I let the tears come,
unashamed and slow,
because love,
real love,
asks for no disguise.

Each drop a hymn,
each sob a breaking chain,
each quiet gasp a vow:
he will know a father
who feels without shame,
a man
who is man enough
to cry.

To be man enough to cry
is to be man enough
to feel—
without apology,
without armor,
without asking permission
to be whole.

First Haircut, First Heartbreak

He sat in the chair,
small fists clenched beneath the cape,
eyes wide as the clippers buzzed to life—
a sound like growing up
too fast.

The first curl fell,
soft as a whisper,
and something ancient in me flinched.
It wasn't just hair—
it was time,
slipping off his shoulders
in quiet tufts.

I saw myself in him then—
a boy on a rusted porch,
knees scabbed,
my father's hands heavy on my shoulders
as the wind carried away
pieces of who I was becoming.
No words.
Only the weight of becoming someone
I hadn't agreed to yet.

He didn't cry.
But I did—

inwardly,
silently—
the way a tree might weep
for its first lost leaf.

Later,
when he found his reflection changed,
he touched his head
like a question,
like he wasn't sure
where the boy in the mirror had gone.

That night,
he wouldn't sleep.
Said he missed his hair,
said it felt wrong,
said he didn't know why
he felt so sad.

And I held him,
not with answers,
but with the ache of knowing—
this was only the beginning
of the beautiful undoing,
the many little deaths
that shape a life.

So I whispered to him,
not aloud,
but in the quiet language of fathers—
You are still you.
But now you carry a piece of becoming.

Fatherhood in Fragments

It's never whole,
this work of being a father.
It comes in pieces—
morning cereal poured too quickly,
a sock pulled on backwards,
a scraped knee kissed
between emails.

Sometimes it's a Lego brick
lodged in my heel
reminding me he was here,
building something
he didn't finish.
Other times, it's a question
I'm not ready to answer:

"Do people stop being friends forever?"

I try to be present,
but presence feels
like a scattered language—
half-spoken during homework,
half-lost during commutes,
muttered in the dark
when I check if he's still breathing.

I have no grand speeches,
no blueprint carved in stone—
only these broken moments

stitched together
by effort
and grace.

He won't remember all of it—
just the fragments.
But I pray
they're the right ones.
The ones that say:
I stayed.
Even when the world
pulled at me from every side,
I stayed.

Holding My Son After the Sirens

The night split open
with the sound of sirens—
not near, but near enough
to make me gather him
from his dreams.

He didn't wake,
just sighed against my chest,
his breath
a fragile thread of peace
I didn't know I needed to count.

I held him like a prayer
I didn't know how to finish—
tight enough to feel his heartbeat,
gentle enough not to stir his sleep.
In that moment,
I became more shelter than man.

Outside,
the world was proving again
how quickly safety unravels.
Another name.
Another mother's scream
rising into the night air—
a psalm of grief

too loud to ignore.

I whispered that name,
folded now
into mourning,
into marches,
into a list too long
for any lullaby.

But here,
in this quiet room,
I held onto what I could:
his warmth,
his softness,
the rise and fall of innocence
not yet broken
by the headlines.

I thought of my father—
how he might have stood
in the same darkness,
holding me
against the trembling unknown,
offering nothing
but presence
and the vow
to be there
when the world was not.

I didn't cry,
but something in me knelt—
as if prayer
wasn't what you say,
but what you do
when the world is on fire

and your hands
can only hold
one small life
at a time.

So I stayed,
anchored in his sleep,
watching the sky
for the return of quiet,
whispering promises
I wasn't sure I could keep
but needed to try.

And when he stirred,
half-lost in a dream,
he said one word—
Daddy—
and the storm outside
felt a little less final.

A Letter to the Ones Who Look Like Me

To the ones who look like me—
with eyes that carry questions,
with skin that history has both honored
and hunted,
with names the world mispronounces
until they learn to whisper them in fear—

I see you.

Not just the strength,
but the softness you hide
because someone told you
you had to.

I see the way you walk into rooms
like you're not sure
if you're welcome,
how you smile
just enough
not to be mistaken for threat.

Let me say this plain:
You are not a problem to solve.
You are a promise—
a breath still becoming,
a story that didn't end

with chains
or statistics
or silence.

You are allowed
to be brilliant,
to be broken,
to be both.

You can cry
and not crumble.
You can ask for help
and still be a man.
You can love deeply
without apology.
And when the world
tries to define you
by its fear,
remember:
your existence is already
a kind of resistance.

I write this as someone
still learning,
still healing,
still trying to be
what I didn't always have.

So take your time.
Take your space.
Take the crown
even if no one
hands it to you.

And know this—

you are not alone.
You never were.
You never will be.

Signed,
A man who looks like you,
and loves you enough
to believe
you'll rise further
than I ever could.

The Shadow He Follows

Sometimes
I watch him walk ahead of me,
small shoes tapping
in rhythms not yet weighted
by the world.

And yet—
there it is:
my stride in his step,
my silence in his quiet stare,
my anger
when the puzzle won't fit,
my retreat
when too many eyes are on him.

He doesn't know
the shape of the shadow
that stretches behind him—
the one I've tried to outrun,
reshape,
rename.

But I see it,
feel its breath
on both our necks.
It's mine.
And it's my father's too—
the echo of a man
I barely knew

but still
somehow became.

So I watch closely,
not just him
but myself
walking beside him.
And I wonder:
if I change my step,
can the shadow soften?
Can I be
light
instead of weight?

Sometimes
he turns and smiles,
and for a moment,
I believe—
he's following something brighter
than what followed me.

...But he walks inside it,
light carving my outline
onto his every motion.
What I do not say
becomes his unspoken.
What I swallow
becomes his hunger.

I wanted to raise him
free of my ghosts—
but I see him tracing
their outlines
on bedroom walls
when the night is too still.

So now,
I unlearn the silence.
I speak when it hurts.
I hold him
when I'd rather disappear.
I show him
where the shadow ends
and where the light can begin.

Because he follows,
yes—
but he will also learn
how to step beyond me.

Becoming the Father I Never Met

I built him
from absence—
stitched together
from stories my mother told
in softened tones
and old photographs
where his smile
never quite reached me.

I searched the curve of my hands
for his,
the echo of his voice
in my own
when I first said
"I'm here,"
not just to a child,
but to a vow.

There were no lessons passed down—
no whispered warnings
while changing a tire,
no nod across the room
that meant
you're doing alright.
So I made my own.
At night,

I held my son
the way I hoped
he might have held me—
not tightly,
but wholly.
Not perfectly,

but present.
I am learning
how to show up
without a blueprint,
how to say "I love you"
out loud
and often,
so it doesn't have to be searched for
in silence.

Maybe legacy
isn't what's left behind
but what's made
in the middle
of the mess,
the mystery,
and the choosing.

And so,
each time my child
calls me "Dad"
without flinching,
without wondering
if I'll answer—
I become
the father
I never met.

Teaching Strength Without the Mask

I used to think strength
meant silence—
a jaw locked tight,
a spine that never bent,
hands that never trembled
even beneath the weight.

But my son watches
with wide, waiting eyes,
learning not from what I say
but from the tension I hide
in the space between words.

So I begin again—
I teach him that strength
is not the absence of breaking
but the courage
to name what bends you.

I let him see my weariness,
my joy,
my confusion—
each emotion a page
in the manual I never had.

He asks why I breathe deep

before I speak,
why sometimes
my hands stay open
even when I'm angry.
I tell him:
it's because power
doesn't have to clench its fist
to be real.

We speak of fear
as something we face,
not something we bury.
Of pain
as something we honor,
not something we dodge.

And in the quiet after,
when he curls beside me
like a question mark
in need of no answer,
I know I've begun the work—
of raising a boy
who won't need a mask
to feel whole.

What It Means to Be Called "Daddy"

It's not the word itself—
two syllables
tumbled out with sticky fingers
and sleepy breath—
it's what echoes behind it.

A call for safety
wrapped in sound,
a claim staked
on your presence,
on the way your shadow stretches
across nightmares
and playgrounds alike.

"Daddy" means
you are the first sky they name,
the hands they expect to hold
the world steady.
It means
you have become
both fortress and field—
where they run to hide,
and where they run free.

It is not always gentle.
It is not always earned

on the days when your voice frays
and your patience disappears
beneath the weight of your own storms.

But still—
they say it.
"Daddy."
Like grace.
Like it's never in question.

And in that word
is a mirror:
a reminder
that love doesn't wait
for you to be perfect—
just present.
That being there,
even trembling,
even tired,
still counts.
That hands which don't always know
how to fix the world
can still hold it
gently,
for someone small enough
to believe you can.

Last Will, First Word

If I leave nothing else,
let it be this:
the sound of my voice
reading you into sleep,
the weight of my hand
steadying your first steps,
the way I looked at you
as if wonder had a name.

Let it be
the softness I fought to keep,
the quiet strength
I built from broken men,
the silences I filled
with presence,
not perfection.

Let it be
the way I knelt to your eye level,
answered your cries
without fear of tenderness,
spoke truth gently,
even when it trembled.

Let it be
the softness I fought to keep,
the tears I never hid,
the stories I told you
not just to teach—

but to stay close
even when the world
pulled us apart.

Let it be
the apology I whispered
without needing to be right,
the time I turned back
when the world demanded forward,
the embrace
when I had no answers—
just arms.

You won't find
land deeds or gold.
But you will find
notes in the margins
of your favorite books,
a coat that still smells
like pine and sweat,
a silence that never felt
like absence.

And maybe,
when you speak my name
to your child one day,
it won't be legacy
you pass down—
but a first word,
fresh as breath,
carved from love
I once held
in my hands.

Not a monument,

not a myth,
but a memory alive
in the way you kneel
to tie a shoe,
or stay
just five minutes longer
at the bedside
of a restless child.

Let them say,
not that I was strong,
but that I stayed.
Not that I knew,

The Cross and the Crown

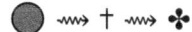

*Ministry was never about perfection—
only presence.
And redemption,
I've learned,
does not shout.
It survives.*

Grace in the Gutter

I found God
not in the stained-glass hush
of sanctuaries,
but in the cracked concrete
where syringes bloom
like rusted lilies
and voices fray into trembling air.

A woman with smoke in her eyes
said Jesus loves me anyway
as if daring me
to believe her.
And I did.
Because her hands
were trembling with truth
the way pulpits never do.

Down there,
where Sunday suits turn to ash
and names are traded
for glances and coins,
grace didn't knock.
It sat beside the broken
and bled with them.

I saw a preacher in withdrawal
reciting Psalms between shivers.
I saw a child
trace a cross

in the dirt with a stick—
no steeple above,
just sky.

If you want to know redemption,
don't start with the saved.
Go where mercy
isn't clean or quiet,
where hope smells like sweat
and sounds like
I made it through another night.

That's where I found it.
Not above,
but beneath.
In the gutter—
grace.
Or maybe
it found me.
Maybe that's the only place
I could finally see it—
because that's where I was.
Not reaching up,
but laid low,
sprawled in the wreckage
of my own undoing,
too tired to pretend
I was clean.

Preacher with a Past

They see the collar now,
hear the cadence in my voice,
feel the weight of Scripture
when I speak—
but they don't know
about the nights
I preached to myself
in back alleys
with whiskey on my breath
and shame dripping from my coat.

Before I stood in pulpits,
I stood in courtrooms.
Before I wore robes,
I wore records—
the kind that don't get sealed,
just judged
in whispers.

I don't preach from perfection.
I preach from the pit.
From the bottom of bottles,
from silence that lasted too long,
from fists that shook
because I didn't know
how to pray
without being angry first.

They say God uses the broken,

but they never talk about
how long it takes
to believe you're worthy of being held.
They never tell you
that grace doesn't always come
with applause—
sometimes it limps.
Sometimes it stares at its own reflection
and doesn't flinch.

So yes, I preach.
But not to be admired.
I preach
because I know what it is
to be lost—
and to be found
without deserving it.

So yes, I preach.
But not to be admired.
I preach
because I know what it is
to be lost—
and to be found
without deserving it.

I preach
because some Sundays,
I still feel the weight
of who I used to be
climbing into the pulpit with me.
And I let him.

Because redemption
ain't about erasing the past—

it's about walking with it
and letting the light hit it
from a new direction.

Some days,
the sermon is for me.
To remind myself
that grace doesn't skip over
those who fell hardest.
It dwells there.
It builds altars
where shame once stood.

And when I raise my hands,
it's not to say
"look at me."
It's to say—
He brought me through,
and if He brought me through,
He can reach you too.

The Altar in My Chest

I don't need stained glass
to find God.
He meets me
in the hollow of my chest,
where prayers rise
before words form,
where grief has carved
its own liturgy.

There is an altar there—
not made of gold,
but of scar tissue,
held together
by memories that still ache
but no longer define me.

I've knelt in churches
that forgot my name,
sat in pews
while folks praised louder
than they lived.
But in the stillness
between breath and breaking,
I learned:
worship is not a performance—
it's presence.
And I carry it
with me.

This heart—
this cracked vessel—
still opens like a sanctuary.
Still burns
with quiet offerings
no one else sees.
Still believes
that even broken bread
can be holy.

And when the world tells me
I need a steeple to be whole,
I press my hand to my chest
and feel it beating—
the altar still there,
still burning,
still enough.

Sunday Morning After the Riot

The sanctuary smelled like smoke,
not incense—
ash clung to the choir robes,
glass shimmered like shattered halos
on the blood-washed steps.
We gathered anyway.
Hymns rose
from throats still hoarse
from chanting justice
the night before.

The pastor's collar was crooked,
his voice cracked
on every "Amen."
No organ played.
The piano was scorched,
but the Spirit—
the Spirit showed up barefoot,
grimy,
and still good.

We didn't dress up.
We came as we were—
bandaged,
bruised,
carrying signs

and stories
and the rage
we weren't allowed
to call holy.

The sermon wasn't in the pulpit.
It was in the silence
between our bowed heads.
It was in the child
still rocking in her mother's lap,
too young to protest,
too sacred to ignore.

Some cried.
Some stared out the broken windows
as if expecting God
to walk through the smoke.
But He already had.
Last night.
In the streets.
In the screams.
In the ones who stayed
to sweep up glass
even after the news cameras left.

And on this morning—
this raw, holy morning—
we didn't need revival.
We needed remembrance.
And a gospel
that knew how to bleed.

Gospel for the Wounded

This ain't the gospel of clean hands
and perfect attendance.
This is the gospel
for those who've bled quietly
in the back pew,
who've wept through altar calls
and still limped home
unhealed.

It's for the ones
who know how to worship
with cracked voices,
who carry grief
like scripture,
who show up
not because they feel holy—
but because they're still breathing.

This is gospel
for the bruised,
the doubters,
the ones who've prayed,
then cursed,
then prayed again.
The ones who've buried brothers
and held mothers
while the verdict read
"not guilty."

It doesn't promise
you won't break.
It promises
you won't break alone.

It doesn't erase the pain.
It sings through it.
It walks beside you
on the nights
when even hope
has gone quiet.

This gospel don't shout.
It listens.
It sits beside the addict,
the outcast,
the man who hasn't told anyone
he's falling apart.

It is a gospel
stitched from the torn hem
of survival.
Not polished—
but possible.
Not triumphant—
but true.

Crown of Bruised Gold

They expect a king
without scars,
a crown without weight,
a victory
that never walked through the valley.

But I wear mine tilted—
not out of pride,
but because pain
rearranged my posture.
Because some of us
learned to stand
while still bleeding.

My crown
ain't diamonds and shine—
it's cracked teeth,
tear-soaked prayers,
a thousand nights
spent losing battles
that still led me here.

It was shaped
by the fists I never threw,
the words I never swallowed,
the moments I didn't die
when I thought I would.
It was forged
in silence,

anointed in sweat,
and set upon my head
by a God who saw fit
to crown the ones
who kept walking
even when no one was watching.

They call it bruised
like it's broken.
But I know better.
Gold don't lose its worth
just because it's been through the fire.

I wear this crown
for every man
who was told he'd never rise—
and did.
Not to be praised,
but to remind the world
what resilience looks like
after resurrection.

I Preach with a Limp

Don't let the cadence fool you.
I didn't come to this pulpit
from the mountain—
I crawled out of a ditch,
dragging the gospel
through the mud
of my own undoing.

I preach with a limp
because I've wrestled
with God
and my guilt
and the ghosts
of who I could've been.
And I walked away—
not whole,
but held.

My sermons carry
the scent of smoke,
the weight of nights
when I begged heaven
to say something
other than wait.
I don't speak from power.
I speak from the scar
that never quite closed.

There are Sundays

I barely make it to the mic.
But I show up.
With grief still clinging to my ankles,
and mercy
brushing the dust from my shoulders.

And when I say "grace,"
know this—
I'm not reciting.
I'm remembering.
Because grace met me
limping toward the light,
ashamed and unsure,
and still said,
Stand.

So I preach.
Not because I'm healed,
but because I'm healing.
Because somebody needs to know
you don't have to be whole
to be called.

Miracles in Minor Keys

Not every miracle sings in major.
Some arrive
in cracked harmonies,
barely heard above the noise
of ordinary grief.

Some look like
a man rising
from his own failure,
like breath returning
after too many days of silence.

I've seen deliverance
in a whisper,
salvation
in the way a child
forgave me
before I ever asked.

The choir doesn't always shout.
Sometimes,
it hums low—
a note carried
in the chest
like a question,
like maybe today
I'll make it through.

I've learned to listen

for God
in the offbeat.
In cracked voices,
in sorrow-soaked pews,
in the small hallelujahs
mumbled between sighs.

Because joy
ain't always loud.
And mercy
don't always rhyme.
But it's there—
in the blues,
in the breakdown,
in the silence
right before the next verse.

I've stopped waiting
for thunder.
Now I watch for the light
that flickers
but refuses to die.
That, too,
is a miracle.

The God Who Listens to Broken Men

Not the polished ones—
not the ones with perfect prayers
and rehearsed amens.
I'm talking about the men
who stutter grace,
who show up late
with heavy eyes
and heavier hearts.

The ones who stand
in the back of the church,
unsure if the altar
is meant for men
who've been arrested,
abandoned,
or just angry too long
to know the sound of peace.

I've seen them—
heads bowed like broken streetlights,
hands shoved deep in pockets
like they're holding back
everything they were never allowed
to feel out loud.

And still,

God listens.
Not just to their words,
but to their sighs,
their silence,
their shoulders sagging under history
and the hush of generational pain.

He hears the prayer
that doesn't rise,
the faith
that barely flickers,
the name uttered
only when no one's around.

And He doesn't flinch.

He listens—
like a Father who knows
His son won't call Him
until he's at the end
of his rope,
but still picks up
on the first ring.

I know,
because I've prayed
from the floor,
from the back seat of a squad car,
from hospital rooms
and courtrooms
and the corner
of a childhood bedroom
where I thought
no one heard.

But He did.
Still does.
And that's why I'm here—
not whole,
but heard.

Pulpit in the Projects

I didn't need a steeple
to be called.
Didn't need stained glass,
just the light cutting through
broken blinds
on a Tuesday afternoon.

The first sermon I preached
wasn't in a church—
it was on the corner
next to a man
rolling dice
with Psalm 23
tattooed on his neck.
He said,
Preach something real,
so I did.

No robes,
just a hoodie.
No offering plate,
just pockets full of stories
and a voice
that shook
when I said grace
like I meant it.

The sanctuary was concrete.
The choir was car alarms,

sirens,
and a baby crying upstairs.
Still,
God came.
He always does.

Because holiness
ain't confined to buildings.
It breathes
in basketball courts
and barbershops,
in stairwells where boys
pass blunts and burdens,
in kitchens where mamas
hum spirituals
over frying pans and past-due bills.

This pulpit?
It's a porch,
a park bench,
a stoop where I remind them—
you don't have to leave the block
to find salvation.

You just have to believe
that God speaks
in the dialect of survival,
and still
calls it sacred.

Sermons from the Street

They say the streets don't teach,
but I've learned scripture
from storefront windows,
graffiti walls,
and the eyes of men
who ain't been in a pew
since their mama passed.

I've heard sermons
in sneaker prints
on rain-slicked sidewalks,
in the rhythm of kids
beating buckets like drums
because nobody gave them
real instruments—
just hunger
and time.

There's gospel
in the way a brother says,
You good?
with no smile,
just presence.
In the way we mourn
without ceremony—
candles,
a T-shirt,
a name we chant
until heaven answers.

I've stood in pulpits
with broken benches
and no mic—
just my voice
and the weight of stories
that never made the news
but made me a minister
anyway.

Not licensed,
but called.
Not ordained,
but kept.

The streets don't need
another lecture.
They need a love
that walks with them,
a grace that don't judge
the sag in a man's jeans
or the track marks
on his past.

I preach where the Spirit lands—
and sometimes
it lands on concrete
still warm
from the last fight.

I Gave Them Bread, They Wanted Wine

I brought them what I had—
words torn from long nights
and dry prayers,
crumbs of faith
I'd gathered
from the edges of my own hunger.

I gave them bread,
the kind that sustains,
the kind that's not sweet
but steady—
daily,
quiet,
like love that stays
even when it's not praised.

But they wanted wine.
They wanted celebration,
miracles in full color,
a gospel dressed in glitter,
something that sparkled
when they swallowed it.

They didn't want the slow work
of healing—
they wanted hallelujahs

without the hurt.
Wanted to sip joy
without first tasting
the dirt it came from.

And still—
I gave what I had.
Broke myself open
like loaves
in the hands of One
who knows how to multiply
what feels like not enough.

They may not remember the meal.
But maybe,
one day,
when the wine runs out
and their souls grow faint,
they'll remember
the bread.
The plain,
torn,
still-warm mercy
I placed into their hands.

Where Faith Feels Like Fury

Some days,
I don't lift my hands in worship—
I raise my fists.
Not to fight God,
but to remind Him
I'm still here.
Still trying.
Still angry
in a world that makes belief
feel like betrayal.

There are prayers
I've shouted into the dark
with more heat than hope.
There are verses
I've thrown across the room
because they promised peace
and I couldn't find any.

Faith, for me,
has never been passive.
It's been protest.
It's been screaming why?
while still showing up
on Sunday.
It's been walking toward heaven
with blistered feet
and clenched jaw.

And still—
I believe.
Not because it's easy,
but because I've seen too much
to quit.
Because beneath the fire,
there's still a flicker
that won't die.

This isn't the faith
they preach in quiet chapels.
It's the kind that riots
against despair.
The kind that keeps
marching,
crying,
healing,
even when God feels
just out of reach.

It's sacred.
It's survival.
It's mine.

Judas Was My Brother

He didn't wear horns.
Didn't hiss when he walked in.
He knew my kids,
ate at my table,
called me brother
with a voice I trusted.

That's the thing—
betrayal don't always shout.
Sometimes it whispers
in familiar tones,
uses your first name
like a blessing
before turning the blade.

He didn't sell me for silver,
just for silence,
for safety,
for a seat at a table
I wasn't invited to.
And still—
I loved him.
Still prayed
he'd come back
before the garden
went dark.

But the truth is,
some brothers don't return.

Some hand you over
because they can't handle
the weight of your calling,
or the light
you refuse to dim.

And what hurts the most
is not the betrayal—
it's knowing you'd still
have washed his feet.
Still called him friend.
Still made room
for him at the last supper
of your trust.

I forgave him.
Not because he asked,
but because I had to—
to live,
to lead,
to keep loving
without locking every door.

Judas was my brother.
And somewhere
beneath the sting,
I still hope
his soul found grace.

Praise Without Performance

I don't clap on cue anymore.
Don't dance just because the organ says so.
I've learned to praise
without the polish,
without the pressure
to make it pretty for the crowd.

Some Sundays,
my hallelujah comes out hoarse—
a cracked whisper
from beneath the weight of another week.
Some days,
I don't lift my hands—
I lift my eyes
and that's enough.

I was taught
that praise had to sound like joy,
look like power,
move like victory.
But I've praised
with tears in my mouth
and doubt in my chest.
I've praised
while grieving,
while healing,
while wondering
if God heard me at all.

And still—
I praise.

Not for applause.
Not for validation.
But because something
in me
still reaches
even when nothing answers.
Because sometimes,
the truest praise
is showing up
without the need to be seen.
Just standing.
Just breathing.
Just being.

That, too, is holy.

The Church Hurt Too

They talk about church hurt
like the church is just the cause—
but nobody asks
how many pews have wept,
how many pulpits cracked
under the weight
of silent suffering.

I've seen it—
the deacon who always smiles
but hasn't felt God in years,
the usher with hands steady on the door
but trembling in her spirit,
the pastor preaching
to a room full of people
who never ask
if he's still bleeding.

Yes, the church hurt me—
but I hurt it too.
With my absence,
my pride,
my need to perform healing
instead of living it.

We come here
wounded and waiting,
expecting the stained glass
to know how to hold us.

But the church is made of people—
bruised,
burned,
and still believing.

Sometimes grace
has a limp.
Sometimes love
needs more than one altar call
to resurrect.

And maybe
we're all the woman
reaching for the hem
and the crowd
pretending not to see her.
Maybe we're all
both healer
and hurt.

But still—
we gather.
Not because we're whole,
but because we remember
that even broken bread
can feed a multitude.

Holiness and Hood

Don't let the gold cross fool you—
I still flinch when blue lights flash.
Still check my back
in the barbershop mirror.
Still pray in a voice
that sounds like survival.

I've got Scripture in one pocket,
a folded obituary in the other.
Lost more brothers
than I've buried sins.
Learned early
that holiness ain't about being above—
it's about being among.

I was baptized
in fire escapes and front stoops,
raised on hymns hummed
between cuss words and dice games,
taught to say "amen"
before I even knew
what it meant.

And still—
God came.
Not dressed in white robes,
but in hoodies and house shoes,
through aunties with sharp tongues
and prayers that worked

even when they didn't sound
like the choir's.
I found holiness
in the hood.
In the way we hold each other
through grief,
in the side-eyes that say,
"You good?"
when words won't form.

It's not two worlds.
It's one gospel.
Worn rough
but still radiant.
Because heaven
has always known
how to meet us
right where we are—
between the curb
and the cross.

Healing in the Halftime

They only see the touchdown.
The testimony.
The praise break.
But they don't see the locker room,
where men sit
in silence,
wrapping bruises
they're not allowed to name.

I found healing,
not in the end zone,
but in the halftime—
when the game paused
and nobody asked me to perform.

Just breathe.
Just sit.
Just feel.

There's something sacred
about that in-between.
When the lights dim,
the noise fades,
and you can finally ask,

Am I okay?
I met God there,
not in victory,
but in rest.

In the coach who pulled me aside
and didn't quote Scripture—
just said,
"Take your time, man."

Sometimes healing comes
not in full sermons,
but in nods,
shoulder taps,
a towel thrown over your head
while you cry in private.

We don't talk enough
about halftime holiness—
about the grace
of stopping long enough
to hear your own heartbeat
and remember
it's still yours.

Yes, I'll go back in.
Yes, I'll fight again.
But let me sit
with my wounds for a while
and call that holy, too.

Redemption Ain't Always Loud

It didn't come with trumpets.
No lightning split the sky.
No crowd clapped
when I forgave myself.

Redemption came
on a Tuesday
when I chose to keep breathing,
chose not to curse the day
for starting without joy.

It came
in small things—
folding laundry,
calling my brother back,
not raising my voice
even when I could've.

They think it has to be grand.
Tears at the altar,
spotlights and soaring music.
But mine came
in a whisper—
a quiet yes
to becoming
something more

than what tried to break me.

I didn't shout.
I didn't run the aisles.
I sat still
and let the silence
hold me
without demanding
a performance.

Redemption ain't always loud.
Sometimes it's a soft look
in the mirror.
Sometimes it's walking past
the old corner
without stopping.
Sometimes it's sleep
without shame.

And when I woke up
and didn't hate myself,
that was the hallelujah.
That was the revival.
That was the miracle
they never televised—
but heaven noticed.

Still I Rise to Preach

They counted me out
before I knew I was in.
Said I wasn't polished enough,
was too raw,
too real,
too much scar
and not enough shine.

But I kept rising.
Not with fanfare,
but with a quiet defiance—
the kind born
from getting up
when staying down
felt safer.

I've buried more brothers
than sermons.
Felt grief in my throat
while declaring hope
from pulpits
that still creak
beneath the weight of what we carry.

And still I rise—
not just to speak,
but to stand.
To be counted
among the broken

who still believe
something holy
can come from cracked vessels.

I rise
because someone needs to know
that falling
doesn't void the calling.
That limping
doesn't cancel the light.

I preach
because silence
almost took me once.
And every word I say now
is proof
I made it through
what should've ended me.

This voice
isn't for show.
It's a flame
passed down
from prophets and grandmothers
who taught me
that resurrection
starts with breath—
and ends with purpose.

So yes—
still I rise to preach.
Not because I'm strong,
but because I'm sent.

Sent to speak for the silenced.
Sent to carry what others buried.
Sent to lift what was never laid down.
Sent to hold what still aches in the shadows.
Sent to bear witness with trembling hands.
Sent to say what silence could not keep.
Sent because the fire still burns.
Sent with nothing but breath—and belief.

I am here.
Still rising.
Still preaching.
Not because I have arrived—
but because I remember
what it felt like
to have no one
speaking for me.

So if your voice trembles,
let it tremble loud.
If your hands shake,
let them still reach.
If your scars show,
let them testify.

Because somewhere—
everywhere—
Black men are watching.
Waiting.
For permission
to rise too.

The Poet's Reflection

These poems were written for the moments
we often carry in silence—
the weight behind the nod,
the stories behind the scar,
the breath we hold in rooms
that don't see us.

To the Black men reading this:
This book is not your blueprint—
it's your permission.
Permission to feel deeply,
to grieve fully,
to love without armor,
to speak without asking.

You are not what the world reduced you to.
You are legacy in motion.
Becoming is not weakness;
it is holy work.

I hope you see yourself here—
not just the pain,
but the power.
Let these words be a mirror
and a movement.

Carry them into barber shops,
into Bible studies,
into classrooms,
into quiet corners.

Let them open doors you forgot were closed.

For those who don't look like me:
I hope these poems offer not just awareness,
but understanding.
Read them not as testimony from afar,
but as a hand extended.
May empathy become practice.

This book is a body.
May you walk with it gently.

— *John David Smith*

The Blessing

May these pages find you
where your silence aches most—
and sit beside it,
not to fix,
but to witness.

May you remember
that your story matters,
even when the world
misspells your name
or forgets your light.

May the wounds you carry
become wisdom,
the shadows you've walked through
become shelter for another.

May your voice—
trembling or thunderous—
be received
as sacred.
And if you ever doubt
that your breath is holy,
read these lines again.
Let them be mirror,

be mercy,
be reminder:

You are still here.
You are still becoming.
And that
is a miracle.

— *John David Smith*

Notes for the Curious

● ⟿ † ⟿ ✤

Brief reflections and cultural footnotes
to accompany the journey

What My Name Wasn't

Names like Malik, Kofi, Elijah, and others used throughout this collection are sacred. They carry stories, roots, and rhythms often reshaped or erased in colonial or Western mouths.

When you read them, say them with care. Speak them like prayer—complete, uncut, as they were given.

The Knock at Midnight

An echo of Dr. King's sermon by the same name. "Midnight" is both literal and spiritual—when justice sleeps and fear stands at the door.

Barbershop Baptism

A rite of passage. In the Black barbershop, identity is edged and affirmed—haircut as inheritance, chair as altar.

Code-switching

The art of switching dialects, posture, and presence to survive in spaces not built for you. Fluency in disguise.

First Sunday Suit

The tradition of wearing your best for church—an act of dignity, worship, and resistance, passed through generations.

Shoelaces and Silence

Father absence, unsaid questions, and the quiet instruction of becoming a man without a map.

Permission to Hurt

To feel fully. To name pain without apology. A reclamation of the right to grieve out loud.

Crossed Legs. Clenched Fists

Respectability is a performance. Sometimes stillness is mistaken for peace—while rage smolders beneath the table.

The Prophet in Me Trembled

Prophetic voices often shake. Speaking truth costs something. To tremble and speak anyway is holy.

In My Shadow

A meditation on inherited trauma, racial memory, and the ghosts that walk beside Black boys as they grow.

The Voice I Borrowed

The long path to an authentic voice often begins with mimicry. Especially when your own voice has been questioned.

The Fragile Hallelujah of Black Love

Love under pressure. A portrait of what it means to hold tenderness inside a storm.

This Ain't My Cross—But I Carry It

The burdens of systemic racism are inherited, not chosen. This is about carrying weight with dignity that was never yours to hold.

Alphabet of Survival

A poetic primer in the unspoken lessons Black children learn early: how to exist, endure, and adapt.

The Mirror in My Grandfather's Hallway

Family legacy lives in reflection. Sometimes mirrors don't speak, but they show us the lineage we wear on our face.

Thunder Without Rain

Pent-up rage. Suppressed grief. The sound of storm in a body that has not yet been allowed to break.

Spirits in the Cotton

Ancestral presence in the land. The ghosts that still hum where blood was buried and harvest came too late.

I Prayed in a Language I Never Learned

Spiritual memory that predates words. Sometimes the body remembers what the mouth forgot.

Psalms from My Bones

Worship doesn't always wear robes. Praise sometimes lives in the ache, the breath, the silent endurance of the body.

Every Scar Is Scripture

Scars are holy text. The body carries testimony where words cannot go. To heal is to preach without speaking.

Legacy in the Lullaby

Fathers pass on more than genes. Sometimes it's a hum, a glance, a hush that teaches what strength really is.

Reflection Guide
for Discussion & Teaching

● ⋙ † ⋙ ❖

For Small Groups, Classrooms, or Book Clubs

Before They Called Me Boy

What part of your identity was shaped by others before you fully understood yourself?

The Mirror in My Grandfather's Hallway

What reflections from your elders still live in you today?

Cuffed for Breathing

How does silence serve—or fail—you in the face of injustice?

Man Enough to Cry

What messages were you given about masculinity and emotion growing up?

I Preach with a Limp

What wounds still speak through you, and where has grace met your pain?

In My Shadow

How does generational trauma or memory shape the way you walk through the world?

The Smile They Feared

Has your presence ever been misunderstood as threat?
How did that shape you?

When Brothers Betray

Have you ever been wounded by someone you trusted?
What did you learn from that?

The Prophet in Me Trembled

What truth do you carry that you're afraid to speak?
Why does it matter?

Unarmed, Unseen, Unforgiven

What does it mean to be invisible and still viewed as
dangerous?

Permission to Hurt

What emotions have you been told you're not allowed
to express?

Crossed Legs, Clenched Fists

How have you mastered the art of hiding your pain or
power?

Indicted By Hue

How has skin color affected your experiences, assumptions, or opportunities?

The Knock at Midnight

What "midnight moments" have shaped your faith or urgency to act?

The Shadow He Follows

What are you modeling for those who look up to you, knowingly or not?

The Fragile Hallelujah of Black Love

What does it mean to love boldly in the midst of generational pain?

This Ain't My Cross—But I Carry It

What burdens do you carry that were never meant to be yours?

The Language of Less Than

In what ways have you been taught to shrink yourself? How do you resist that now?

We Rise Anyway

Despite everything, how have you kept rising? What still fuels your resilience?

The Blessing They Didn't Expect

What does it mean to be a blessing in a world that didn't expect you to survive?

Want a printable version of this guide, bonus
questions, and teaching tools?
Scan the QR code or visit:
www.scribeandcanvas.com/resources

*Created for educators, book clubs, spiritual
communities, and sacred conversations.*

www.ingramcontent.com/pod-product-compliance
Lightning Source LLC
Chambersburg PA
CBHW051611120626
46551CB00014B/1749